LIVING BEYOND THE NORM

LIVING
BEYOND THE NORM

28 DAYS TO CHANGE THE WAY YOU THINK ABOUT HEALTH AND WHOLENESS

By Shearon A. Brown

XULON PRESS

Xulon Press
2301 Lucien Way #415
Maitland, FL 32751
407.339.4217
www.xulonpress.com

Printed in the United States of America.
ISBN-13: 978-1-6322-1563-5

Isaiah 53:4-5

Common English Bible (CEB)

⁴ It was certainly our sickness that he carried,
and our sufferings that he bore,
but we thought him afflicted,
struck down by God and tormented.
⁵ He was pierced because of our rebellions
and crushed because of our crimes.
He bore the punishment that made us whole;
by his wounds we are healed.

Table of Contents

DEDICATION

This book is dedicated to my mother, the late Vivian Elizabeth Brown–an awesome woman of God, outstanding teacher of the Word of God, and a great woman of faith. I am grateful to my mother for giving me a sound foundation in the Word of God and making the Word of God top priority in our home as described in Deuteronomy 6:6-9 GOD'S WORD Translation (GW).

> *⁶ Take to heart these words that I give you today. ⁷ Repeat them to your children. Talk about them when you're at home or away, when you lie down or get up. ⁸ Write them down, and tie them around your wrist, and wear them as headbands as a reminder.⁹ Write them on the doorframes of your houses and on your gates.*

My mother dedicated most of her life to teaching and praying for people to be healed and whole.

I am so blessed and inspired by my mother's love for God and people, and her passion to see people walk in divine health and wholeness.

ACKNOWLEDGEMENTS

Special thanks to Bishop J. C. Hash, Sr., my pastor, mentor, and spiritual father. Bishop Hash is Senior Pastor of St. Peter's Church and World Outreach Center in Winston Salem, North Carolina. He is a Bible scholar, teacher, author, and mentor to pastors. He is an internationally-known conference speaker and teacher of faith. I am so blessed to have such an awesome spiritual father who gives me spiritual guidance, inspiration, and encouragement to step out in faith to do things which will impact the world for the glory of God.

Thanks to Mrs. Joyce Hash, the First Lady of St. Peter's Church and World Outreach Center, and those in my St. Peter's church family who have encouraged and inspired me.

And lastly, but not least, I give special thanks to Janice Brown Foster, my sister in the Lord and in the natural, for being my best friend, prayer partner and a constant source of inspiration and encouragement.

INTRODUCTION

C onsider the following:
*You are at a point in your life where every moment of
every day, you are aware of a presence surrounding you and
in you. This presence causes you to have a peace that cannot
be explained. You are filled with a joy that energizes your spirit,
soul, and body. When confronted with problems, a voice from
deep within you gives you words of encouragement and com-
fort. When you are frustrated, overwhelmed, disappointed, or
stressed, a voice from within says, "Worry for nothing. You
have help and nothing is impossible." When there is pain,
symptoms or an undesirable diagnosis from the doctor, a voice
from within assures you, saying, "Provision has already been
made for the healing of your body." You have found that the
voice from within always speaks the truth. And as you believe
and rest in the words spoken to you, things always work out for
the good. Now you are to the point that you no longer wrestle
between believing the voice from within or believing voices
from without coming from circumstances, reasonings, feelings, and other sources that are contradicting the voice from
within. You now know that the voice from within is coming from
the Holy Spirit which now resides in you because when you
accepted Jesus as your savior, your body became the temple*

of the Holy Spirit. Now you have a comforter, a helper, and a guide within you who will reveal the truth of God's Word to you. The presence of the Holy Spirit within you even brings life to your mortal body. Now, with all your being, you are giving God ultimate praise because you realize through His presence in your life, you are living a supernatural life – you are living a life beyond the norm!

Did you know that you can live a life beyond what normal people live? Did you know that God wants you to be healthy and whole, and His plan is for you to walk in health which is far beyond what most people experience? God in His infinite wisdom has prepared a glorious life for you. If you are open to His will for your life, you can live a life that is far beyond what most people consider to be normal. There is a higher life – a best life. You cannot afford to settle for less than what God has for you.

Jesus paid a great price so that we could be redeemed from the curse of sickness and diseases. Even before Jesus paid such a great price, He spent a great portion of His earthly ministry healing the sick. Jesus was moved with compassion every time He saw sickness and diseases impacting the lives of people. Jesus spent much of His ministry making people healthy and whole. Jesus was a healer and Jesus is The Healer today.

We live in a fallen world, and there is a real devil. According to John 10:10, the devil comes to steal, kill, and destroy. The devil's goal is to steal our health, kill and destroy our bodies. Many are in battles for their health and wholeness every day. But we must realize that the battle has already been won. Jesus came and destroyed the works of the devil (1 John 3:8). Jesus took stripes on His body that our bodies may be healed (1 Peter 2:24). As born-again believers, our bodies are temples of the Holy Spirit (1 Corinthians 6:19). Just think, we have the same Spirit that raised Jesus' body from the dead living in our bodies, giving life to our mortal bodies (Romans 8:11). Also, according to John 10:10, Jesus came that you might have abundant life. An abundant life is a life of health and wholeness.

It is God's will for all to be well and whole. We can see that this is backed by the very Word of God and the acts of Jesus. If we believe that God's Word is true, we cannot deny that He wants us well and whole in our spirit, our soul, and in our bodies.

We can see that there is a contradiction between what most people experience and what the Word of God promises when it comes to health and wholeness. What most people consider to be the norm is far beneath what God describes in His Word. God's Word provides the standards, and it up to us through faith in His Word to live up to those standards. Living up to God's standards–that is, walking out His will for our lives–is nothing we can do on our own. We must seek God's wisdom and the assistance of the Holy Spirit to carry out His will for our lives.

The Word of God is the absolute truth. If we are not seeing the Word of God manifested in everyday life, we must ask, "Why?" I am a firm believer that God wants us to ask questions. If based on our knowledge and understanding, we are coming up short, we need to know what we are missing. We must seek God for wisdom and revelation on where we are coming up short. Acknowledging we have "missed it" is in no way condemning. Rather, we are humbling ourselves and taking off pride to be open to God to give us wisdom and understanding. When we look at the experiences of most people and conclude that what we see is just the way life is supposed to be, we give God no opportunity to enlighten us and open the eyes of our understanding.

If we ask and diligently seek, we will find the answers to every question that we may have. God wants us to be inquisitive. He wants us to ask Him questions so He can answer, instead of us coming up with answers from our own rational reasoning and perception of things. He wants us to depend on Him for answers. God said, "My people are destroyed for lack of knowledge" (Hosea 4:6). God wants us to have knowledge of His thoughts and have understanding based on His wisdom.

The material that you are about to read is based on a prayer asking for divine revelation on the topic of health and wholeness. The following is my inquisitive prayer for divine revelations:

> *"Lord, why do so many people suffer from sicknesses and diseases, when Jesus has already taken stripes on His body that our bodies may be healed? Why is it that we are not seeing the magnitude of manifestations of healings as in Jesus' earthly ministry and in the ministry of the early church? Show us what we have missed. Show us our misconceptions. We know if there is*

any shortcoming, it is in us, not in You. What are we not seeing? Let us know what we are doing to inhibit health and wholeness in our lives and what are we not doing to promote health and wholeness in our lives. Lord, help us to line up with Your Word so that there will be a manifestation in our lives of what You have spoken in Your Word. I pray in agreement with Ephesians 1:17-20 (TPT),

- *I pray that the Father of glory, the God of our Lord Jesus Christ, would impart to us the riches of the Spirit of wisdom and the Spirit of revelation to know him through our deepening intimacy with him.*
- *I pray that the light of God will illuminate the eyes of our imagination, flooding us with light, until we experience the full revelation of the hope of his calling—that is, the wealth of God's glorious inheritances that he finds in us, his holy ones!*
- *I pray that we will continually experience the immeasurable greatness of God's power made available to us through faith. Then our lives will be an advertisement of this immense power as it works through us! This is the mighty power that was released when God raised Christ from the dead and exalted him to the place of highest honor and supreme authority in the heavenly realm!*

I pray this in Jesus' Name. Amen!

This book consists of bits of revelation given to me, of which I believe to be pieces of the puzzle creating the answer to the inquisitive prayer that I just shared with you. This book is to enlighten individuals to not to settle for the normal way of living, but instead to operate in a level of health and wholeness that is beyond what most people experience. In addition to the natural things that we do to promote health and wholeness, we who are born-again believers have supernatural assistance enabling us to operate at a level of health and wholeness that is beyond the norm.

We must seek God's knowledge and wisdom through His Word and not just think that our experiences or the experiences of most people is God's will for our lives. By seeking God, I found that His Word has so much to say about health and wholeness. Many of the things God revealed to me through His Word are in this book. This book focuses on the health and wholeness of the body; but we cannot talk about the health and wholeness of the body without talking about wholeness of the spirit and soul. As humans, we are spirit, we have a soul (mind, will, emotions), and we live in a body. The condition of the spirit and soul greatly impacts the body. We will discuss how the Holy Spirit and the Word of God work together to bring wholeness to the spirit, soul and body.

Join me on this exciting adventure of following the Holy Spirit as He reveals wisdom and understanding concerning living a life of health and wholeness that is beyond the norm.

For those who are inquisitive, may you find this to be the beginning of your own quest for seeking wisdom and revelation from our Father God. There is so much He wants us to know, so stay inquisitive and become a wisdom-seeker.

It is God's will for all to walk in a level of health and wholeness that is beyond what most people experience. According to 1 Corinthians 2:9-10, "Eye has not seen, nor ear heard, nor have entered into the heart of man the things which God has prepared for those who love Him. But God has revealed them to us through His Spirit." As we seek God's wisdom, we can trust that God will reveal to us through His Spirit exactly how to carry out His will in living a life beyond the norm.

How to Use This Book

This book is designed to coach you in a twenty-eight-day process to change the way you think about health and wholeness. There are twenty-eight topics. You are expected to read and meditate on one topic each day. Each topic presents a Biblical viewpoint on living in health and wholeness that is beyond the norm and is accompanied by a prayer and a confession to assist you in meditating on the principle presented on the topic. Finally, there is a page available to record your personal thoughts about that day's topic.

The first twelve days focus on developing a lifestyle which promotes divine health and wholeness. Days thirteen through fifteen give tools to use in fighting for your health and wholeness. Days sixteen through twenty-one identify enemies to walking in divine health and wholeness. Days twenty-two through twenty-six concentrate on Biblical foundations for divine health and wholeness. And days twenty-seven and twenty-eight give some final thoughts and insights.

For best results, I suggest that you read this book over and over again. I recommend reading it at least three times to get these nuggets of truth not just as head knowledge, but down into your heart, empowering you to develop a lifestyle of walking in health and wholeness that is beyond the norm.

A Lifestyle of Divine Health and Wholeness

Jesus said in John 10:10

The Passion Translation (TPT) "... **I have come to** *give you everything in abundance, more than you expect*—**life in its fullness until you overflow!**"

New Living Translation (NLT) "... **My purpose is to give them a rich and satisfying life.**"

Amplified Bible (AMP) "... **I came that they may have** *and* **enjoy life, and have it in abundance [to the full, till it overflows].**"

DAY 1

Envision Yourself Strong and Healthy

Scriptures:

> **Numbers 13:33–**... *and we were in our own sight as grasshoppers...*

> *2 Corinthians 10:5 Modern English Version (MEV)–casting down imaginations and every high thing that exalts itself against the knowledge of God, bringing every thought into captivity to the obedience of Christ,*

What vision do you have of yourself? Do you see yourself as weak, sickly, and frail? Do you envision a future of declining health, loss of vitality, and sickness and disease dominating your life? If so, you need a new vision, a new perception of yourself!

Are you familiar with the Biblical account of the Children of Israel? Twelve spies were sent to check out the land God had promised them. Ten of the twelve returned with bad reports. In

1

Numbers 13, the ten spies with the bad reports stated, "And we were in our sight as grasshoppers…" They saw themselves as weak and unable to walk into what God had promised them. In His Word, God promised health, strength, youth restoration and a long satisfying life. Do you see yourself possessing what God has promised?

See yourself strong and healthy. **SEE IT! SEE IT! LOOK FOR IT! SEE IT!** This is what I call the "SEE IT! SEE IT! LOOK FOR IT! SEE IT! Revelation." **SEE IT** in the spirit by meditating and believing the Word of God. **SEE IT** in your mind's eye by using your imagination to visualize God's Word being manifested in your body. Once you see it in the spirit and with your imagination, then, **LOOK FOR IT** to manifest in your body. When you look for something, you are expecting it to show up. And as you continue to look for it, expecting, you will **SEE IT** manifested in your body. We are tri-part beings: We are spirit, we have a soul (mind, will and emotions), and we live in a body. For our bodies to be strong and healthy, we must see it in the spirit (in the Word of God), see it with our soul (through our imagination), then, look for it to be manifested in the natural body. When we do, we will see God's promise of health and strength manifest in our body.

According to II Corinthians 10:5, we must cast down imaginations that oppose what God's Word has promised and bring every thought in line with what Jesus has done for us. Jesus has redeemed us from weakness, sickness, and disease. Analyze your thoughts and imaginations concerning your health and wholeness. Get real with yourself. Don't allow any thought or imagination of your being weak or having poor health to linger. Don't meditate on such thoughts. Cast them down immediately! You cast down a thought by boldly speaking what God has promised you in His Word. If there is a thought of you having a sickness or weakness, cast it down immediately by BOLDLY saying, "I refuse to be sick or weak because by Jesus' stripes, I am healed!" When I say, "BOLDLY saying," I mean speak with authority. Luke 10:19 states that God has given you authority over all the power of the enemy, and nothing shall harm you. Sickness and weakness are enemies to your health and wholeness. Therefore, God has given you authority over sickness and weakness.

Refuse to see yourself any way other than what God has promised. Envision yourself strong, healthy, thriving, and full of life.

PRAYER:

Father God, thank you for opening my eyes to see myself the way you see me. I repent for any words or imaginations that I have thought or said of myself as being weak, frail, and unhealthy. Help me to see myself the way you see me – strong, youthful, and whole. I thank You that You love me so much that You made provision for me to be in perfect health by the stripes of Jesus. I pray this in Jesus' Name. Amen!

CONFESSION:

I commit to visualizing myself the way the Word of God describes me. I am strong, healthy, youthful, whole, and full of life. I refuse to see myself any other way.

PERSONAL THOUGHTS:

_____

_____

_____

_____

_____

_____

_____

_____

_____

_____

_____

_____

_____

_____

_____

_____

_____

_____

_____

_____

_____

DAY 2

Present Your Body as A Living Sacrifice

Scriptures:

> *Romans 12:1 (KJV)*–*I beseech you therefore, brethren by the mercies of God, that you present your bodies a living sacrifice, holy, acceptable unto God, which is your reasonable service.*

> *1 Corinthians 6:19-20 (KJV)*–*What? know ye not that your body is the temple of the Holy Ghost which is in you, which ye have of God, and ye are not your own? [20] For ye are bought with a price: therefore, glorify God in your body, and in your spirit, which are God's.*

Romans 12:1 gives us a vital ingredient for walking in supernatural divine health and wholeness. We are to willingly present our bodies to God as living sacrifices. As born-again believers, according to 1 Corinthians 6:19-20, our bodies belong to God. They are no longer our own. Our bodies are

God's property and the temple of the Holy Spirit. God sent his Son Jesus to pay the price to set us free from the dominion of Satan. Even though our bodies now belong to God, He has given us the choice to decide what to do with them. Now that Satan has no dominion over our bodies, we can present them to God as living sacrifices, giving God dominion over our bodies; or, we can choose to allow Satan to continue to have dominion.

When you present your body as a living sacrifice, something supernatural takes place. Your body becomes **holy** and **acceptable** according to Romans 12:1. Holy means that your body is now set apart (dedicated) for God's use. So, what does it mean for your body to be an acceptable sacrifice? We can get insight on this in the Old Testament when animals were sacrificed to God. For the body of an animal to be an acceptable sacrifice, it had to be free of blemishes. According to Malachi 1:8, it had to be a body that was not blind, lame, nor sick. As you persistently maintain your body as a living sacrifice, your body becomes an acceptable sacrifice; therefore, your body becomes healthy and whole without sicknesses or blemishes.

When I present my body to God as a living sacrifice, I am saying, "Lord, this is your body to be used by You to do Your will on earth." I am submitting to God's agenda for my body. I am giving God permission to take my body and work His divine will in and through it.

You must willingly present your body as a living sacrifice to God. God will not exert His will over your body without your permission. God is a gentleman; He does not override your will. You must give God permission to take your body and work His divine will in and through your body. Walking in divine health is a part of His divine will.

Once you give your body as a living sacrifice to God, God is obligated to take care of it. When you don't sacrifice your body to God, you are obligating yourself to be its caretaker. Therefore, you will try to find your own ways to provide for, protect, and heal your body. You must realize that God knows better how to take care of your body than you do. After all, He created it! You can trust God with your body. By presenting your body as a living sacrifice, you are putting it under God's control, safely in His hands. Rest assured, God will take good care of your body beyond anything that you could do on your own.

When you choose to present your body as a living sacrifice to God, you receive what God has prepared for you, and that is health, strength, youthfulness, vitality, wholeness, divine protection, peace, joy, and abundant life. If you choose not to present your body as a living sacrifice to God, you are allowing Satan to continue his dominion over your body. Satan only steals, kills, and destroys. That is, he steals your health, kills your body with sickness, disease and destruction, and ultimately destroys your body. So, as a born-again believer, will you reap the benefits of presenting your body as a living sacrifice to God, or reap the destruction of allowing Satan to continue to dominate your body? The choice is yours!

PRAYER:

Father God, I praise You for paying a great price for my body through Your Son, Jesus. I praise You that I can give my body to You as a living sacrifice, causing Satan to no longer have dominion over it. I praise You that as I present it to You as a living sacrifice, my body is made holy and acceptable. My body is holy in that You have separated it to be used by You. You have made my body an acceptable sacrifice in that You have healed it of all sickness and blemishes. I rejoice and praise You, Father God, that You are using my body for Your glory!

I pray this in Jesus' Name. Amen.

CONFESSION:

Today I present my body as a Living Sacrifice to my Father God. As I do this, God sees it as holy and acceptable. I honor God with my body. This body is no longer my own; it is the temple of the Holy Spirit. The same Spirit that raised Jesus' body from the dead operates *freely* in my body, making it alive. Sin and sickness have no place in my body. By Jesus' stripes, my body is healed, my body is BLESSED, and no part of the curse has any effect on it because Satan no longer has dominion over my body. My body is an instrument God will use to manifest His will on earth as His will is in heaven.

As I maintain my body as a living sacrifice to my Father God, my health and strength are increasing more and more; and, my body is lining up with the words I have just spoken. **I**

FULLY EXPECT, LOOK FOR, AND COMMAND THESE WORDS TO MANIFEST IN MY BODY IN JESUS' NAME.

PERSONAL THOUGHTS:

_____

_____

_____

_____

_____

_____

_____

_____

_____

_____

_____

_____

_____

_____

_____

_____

_____

_____

_____

_____

DAY 3

Supernatural Body Scan

Scriptures:

Romans 8:26-27 (NIV) – *In the same way, the Spirit helps us in our weakness. We do not know what we ought to pray for, but the Spirit himself intercedes for us with groans that words cannot express. 27 And he who searches our hearts knows the mind of the Spirit, because the Spirit intercedes for the saints in accordance with God's will.*

Proverbs 3:5-8 (NIV) – *5 Trust in the LORD with all your heart and lean not on your own understanding; 6 in all your ways acknowledge him, and he will make your paths straight. 7 Do not be wise in your own eyes; fear the LORD and shun evil. 8 This will bring health to your body and nourishment to your bones.*

The Holy Spirit is our helper. According to Romans 8:26-27, the Holy Spirit helps us pray for things that are beyond our knowledge and understanding and to pray in accordance with God's will. Praying in the Spirit (praying in tongues) is a powerful weapon against sickness and disease. Pray in the spirit over your body continually. There is no need to wait until a medical examination reveals an attack on your body before attacking it with prayer. Many think that they must know about an illness before they can pray against the illness. Not so! The Holy Spirit knows all things. Praying in the spirit allows us to pray for illnesses that are not even detectable by medical examination, causing us to be proactive–not just reactive–to sickness and disease that would try to attack our bodies. Everything that is manifested in the physical starts in the spiritual realm. By praying in the spirit and believing God's Word, we can prevent harmful things that are in the spiritual realm from being manifested in the physical realm. We have the power within us to put a stop to anything that attempts to destroy our bodies.

Note that Proverbs 3:5 (NIV) says, *"Trust in the LORD with all your heart and **lean not on your own understanding."*** We are so used to **leaning to our own understanding** which is our rational reasoning and perception of things. In prayer, we can spend much of our time praying in our own understanding. We must realize that we just don't know everything, and we don't need to know about something before we pray about it. We can trust God's knowledge by praying in the Spirit the perfect prayer that fully addresses a problem that is beyond our understanding.

When you pray in the spirit over your body daily, you are doing a supernatural body scan. As you pray in the spirit, visualize the supernatural power of God flowing through your body, correcting and perfecting every cell, organ, tissue, muscle, joint, and bone. When we pray in the spirit, God will heal us of things that we never knew we even had. Don't wait until you are experiencing symptoms, or you are diagnosed with an illness before you pray over your body. Pray daily in the spirit over your body to nip the attacks of sickness in the bud before they fully manifest. When we pray in the spirit, we are not leaning to our own understanding; but, instead, we are trusting the wisdom of God to pray the perfect prayer. According to Proverbs 3:8 (NIV), this brings health to your body and nourishment to your bones.

PRAYER:

Lord, help me to pray the perfect prayer over my body. As I yield my tongue to the Holy Spirit, I am confident that I am praying in line with the wisdom of God which is beyond human wisdom. I now pray in the Spirit, giving my body a supernatural body scan. [*Pray in the tongues, directing your prayer over your body from the top of your head all the way down to the bottom of your feet.*] Lord, I thank You that You have provided the Holy Spirit; therefore, I am able to pray the perfect prayer over my body that is beyond my understanding and the understanding of mere humans. I thank You, Lord, that You have heard and answered my prayer. I pray this in Jesus' Name.

CONFESSION:

I pray in the Spirit over my body because the Holy Spirit knows all things. I am praying beyond my understanding and the understanding of medical science. As I pray in the Spirit over my body, I visualize the supernatural power of God putting things in order – adjusting, correcting, and perfecting every cell, tissue, organ, muscle, joint, and bone. My body is lining up with the perfect will of God. My body is healthy and whole.

PERSONAL THOUGHTS:

_____

_____

_____

_____

_____

_____

_____

_____

_____

_____

_____

_____

_____

_____

_____

_____

_____

_____

_____

DAY 4

Embracing a Relationship with God as Our Father

Scriptures:

> **Genesis 1:27, 28 (KJV)**–*So God created man in his own image, in the image of God created he him; male and female created he them.*
>
> *28 And God blessed them, and God said unto them, Be fruitful, and multiply, and replenish the earth, and subdue it: and have dominion over the fish of the sea, and over the fowl of the air, and over every living thing that moveth upon the earth.*
>
> **Genesis 2:7 (KJV)**–*And the Lord God formed man of the dust of the ground, and breathed into his nostrils the breath of life; and man became a living soul.*

Proverbs 3:5-8 The Passion Translation (TPT) – *Trust in the Lord completely, and do not rely on your own opinions. With all your heart rely on him to guide you, and he will lead you in every decision you make.* ⁶ ***Become intimate with him in whatever you do****, and he will lead you wherever you go.* ⁷ *Don't think for a moment that you know it all,* ***for wisdom comes when you adore him with undivided devotion*** *and avoid everything that's wrong.* ⁸ ***Then you will find the healing refreshment your body and spirit long for.***

Psalm 16:11 (KJV) -*Thou wilt shew me the path of life: **in thy presence is fulness of joy;** at thy right hand there are pleasures for evermore.*

Isaiah 53:4-5 Christian Standard Bible (CSB)–*Yet he himself bore our sicknesses, and he carried our pains; but we in turn regarded him stricken, struck down by God, and afflicted.* ⁵ *But he was pierced because of our rebellion, crushed because of our iniquities; punishment for our peace was on him, and we are healed by his wounds.*

There are many factors that assist in promoting good health, such as maintaining a certain weight, eating nourishing food, exercising regularly, etc. These are all good health goals to achieve, but there is a vital ingredient that promotes good health.

To introduce this vital ingredient, we really need a drum-roll. Are you ready? The vital ingredient that promotes good health is…. EMBRACING A RELATIONSHIP WITH GOD AS OUR FATHER!!! To walk in divine health and wholeness, we must have a divine connection with God through a loving father-child relationship. With this vital ingredient, we will not only walk in good health, but also, we will have the capacity to walk in *divine* health and wholeness. There is a difference between health and wholeness and *divine* health and wholeness. Divine health and wholeness add a supernatural component to our natural ability to walk in health and wholeness. The supernatural component comes from a relationship with God, the creator of our bodies.

To fully explain why embracing our relationship with God is the vital ingredient to good health, we must go back to the creation of mankind. In the beginning, God created mankind in His own image, with His own nature. Adam and Eve had a divine connection with God. According to Genesis 2:7, "God breathed into man the breath of life; and man became a living soul." God was mankind's very life source. Adam and Eve were fully aware of God's presence, and God could fellowship with them continuously. They also had perfect bodies with no sickness, disease, pain, or disorders. They were placed in a beautiful garden where they enjoyed God's presence without having a complex of inferiority or a concept of fear.

We have no idea how long this beautiful relationship between God and mankind continued. But at some point, an intruder whose goal was to break the relationship that mankind had with God entered the garden. Satan, the intruder, used deception to cause mankind to distrust God. As a result of their distrust, Adam and Eve disobeyed God's command. Immediately, their relationship with God changed; and, they became separated from God, their very life source.

You see, mankind was never created to live separated from God. As long as they were in right relationship with God, Adam and Eve had no fear and did not suffer with stress, sickness, diseases, or disasters. All their wants and needs were met. However, when mankind became disconnected from God, their source of life, they instantly died spiritually. Their relationship with God immediately changed. Instead of enjoying God's presence, they were now hiding and fearful of the presence of God (Genesis 3:8). Even though they immediately experienced spiritual death, it took hundreds of years after Adam and Eve were separated from God's presence for death to manifest physically. Gradually their separation from God, who was their very life source, took a toll on their physical bodies; and, they eventually experienced physical death.

Our loving God did not give up on having a close relationship with mankind. He implemented a plan to restore mankind back to their original state; and, God worked His redemptive plan through Jesus. Jesus paid the price for man's disobedience which separated him from God. Now, when we accept Jesus as our Savior, the process is reversed. Our relationship with God is restored. We are no longer separated from Him. We now have that divine connection with Him. We are reconnected to our life source by our new spirit which is recreated in the image of God. We now have spiritual life by being re-born into a father-child relationship with Almighty God as our Father. Now, we can come boldly into the very presence of our loving Father God. As we build our new relationship with our Father God by experiencing His presence more and more, fear diminishes and trust grows; worry and stress diminishes and peace and joy grows; and, the health of our bodies is impacted.

Adam and Eve learned to distrust God by believing Satan's lies. Now, as born-again believers, we have to learn to trust Father God by building our relationship with Him. We build our relationship with our Father God by believing His Word, being in continual fellowship with Him, receiving His love, hearing His voice, and being obedient to His Words. By doing these things, we will live a life of faith in God. This leads to a God-centered life full of joy and peace. The more we spend time in God's presence, the more we get to know Him and trust Him, the more we become like Him, and the more sin and sickness will diminish from our lives. I speak of sin and sickness together because they are both a part of a package deal that Satan sold to Adam and Eve. Before sin, there was no sickness because man lived by the very life that God breathed into him. Sin and sickness are two sides of the same coin. When we allow sin to dominate our lives, we open the door for sickness to dominate us. Based on Isaiah 53: 4 and 5, we, as believers, must realize this – **Just as, Jesus paid the price for our sin, so we don't have to pay it, He bore sickness, so we don't have to bear it.** According to Romans 6:14, sin no longer has dominion over us; therefore, sickness has no dominion over us either.

Our ultimate goal should be to develop a close intimate relationship with our Father God. As we put our primary focus on our relationship with Him, we will find that sin and sickness will no longer dominate our lives; and, we will be able to walk in the dominion that God ordained for us from the beginning.

As we continue to develop our relationship with Him, we will wake up one day and realize that our trust in God has grown to the point that fear, worry and stress have been replaced with peace and joy; and every sickness, disease, pain, and disorder in our bodies has been replaced by divine health and wholeness.

I believe the most precious benefit of being born-again is the awesome privilege to be in the very presence of God 24/7 because the Spirit of God is in us. As a born-again believer, God, our Creator, lives in us. Just think about it – the one who created our bodies lives **in** our bodies! God is always present. We don't have to beg Him to come or pray for His presence. All we need to do is to acknowledge His presence.

I am convinced that the vital ingredient to living a long, strong, healthy, whole, and rewarding life is embracing our relationship with our Father God by staying continually aware of His healing presence.

According to Psalm 16:11, *"Thou wilt show me the path of life: **in thy presence is fullness of joy**; at thy right had there are pleasures for evermore."* This scripture is the secret to the best life we could possibly live. As we acknowledge, celebrate, rest in, and enjoy God's presence, our lives will be filled with joy. As we do this, God becomes an intricate part of our life. We allow Him to become our close companion who is always with us. When we reach the point where we seek to enjoy His presence more than anything else, this is where we are truly healed and made whole.

Based on Proverbs 3:5-8 (The Passion Translation), we are to trust God completely, become intimate with him, adore him with undivided devotion, then you will find the healing refreshment that your body and spirit long for. We should make maintaining a close, intimate relationship with our Father God our number one pursuit in life. In doing so, we will walk into every good thing that God has prepared for us – and that includes fullness of joy, peace that passes understanding, and divine health and wholeness.

PRAYER:

Father God, I am so grateful to You. Thank You for loving me and wanting to be in a relationship with me. Thank You for sending Your son, Jesus, to suffer and die for me so that I can be in a close, intimate, loving relationship with You. Thank You that because of our new relationship, Your presence is in me. I am never alone, and I am never without Your love. Help me to always acknowledge and celebrate Your presence. Thank You for the joy and peace that engulf me when I acknowledge Your presence. Thank You that in Your presence is healing and wholeness for my soul and body. Thank You for providing me with the vital ingredient for walking in divine health and wholeness – a relationship with You!

I pray this in Jesus' Name. Amen!

CONFESSION:

As, a born-again believer, I am embracing my relationship with my Father God by acknowledging His presence! In the presence of my Father God:

- I am an overcomer in every area of my life because the Greater One is in me (1 John 4:4).
- I have no need to fear because my Father God is with me (Isaiah 41:10).
- Anything that would try to harm me must fall and perish in His presence (Psalm 9:3).
- I am filled with joy because in His presence is fullness of joy (Psalm 16:11), and joy is my strength and momentum for life (Nehemiah 8:10).

When I embrace my relationship with my Father God by completely trusting Him, becoming intimate with Him and adoring Him with undivided devotion, I will find the healing and refreshment that my body and spirit long for (Proverbs 3:5-8). Divine health and wholeness for my body comes from embracing my relationship with my Father God.

PERSONAL THOUGHTS:

DAY 5

Your Words Matter

Scriptures:

Proverbs 18:21 Easy-to-Read Version (ERV)—
The tongue can speak words that bring life or death. Those who love to talk must be ready to accept what it brings.

Proverbs 18:21 Good News Translation (GNT)—
What you say can preserve life or destroy it; so you must accept the consequences of your words.

1 Peter 5:8 Modern English Version (MEV)—
Be sober and watchful, because your adversary the devil walks around as a roaring lion, seeking whom he may devour.

Luke 6:45 New King James Version (NKJV)—A
good man out of the good treasure of his heart brings forth good; and an evil man out of the evil

treasure of his heart brings forth evil. For out of the abundance of the heart his mouth speaks.

***Ephesians 4:29 Good News Translation (GNT)**–Do not use harmful words, but only helpful words, the kind that build up and pro-vide what is needed, so that what you say will do good to those who hear you.*

We as humans were created in the image of God. God used words to create the earth. He used words to call things into exis-tence. Just as with God, there is creative power in our words. We can call things into existence with words. According to Romans 10:9, we receive salvation by confessing with our mouth and believing in our heart. This same principle will work for everything that we receive in our lives. Whatever we con-fess with our mouth and believe in our heart, we will receive – good or bad. According to Proverbs 18:21 (ERV), the tongue can speak words that bring life or death.

Our words can set the stage for our health and wholeness or the lack thereof. So, the question to ask yourself is, "What am I believing and saying about my health?" Speaking words that are contrary to the Word of God concerning our health will hinder divine health and wholeness from manifesting in our lives. Check your words and see if you are believing and making comments like these:

"I think I am going to be sick."

"If anybody gets the flu, I will."

"I will never get rid of this pain."

"This disease is something I just must learn to live with."

"My mother died of cancer; I will probably die of cancer, too."

"The doctor says there is no cure for my disease, so I just accept what the doctor says."

"My relatives have short life spans, so I don't expect to live a long life."

"As I am getting older, I expect to have more aches and pains."

People are believing and speaking words like these every day without realizing the creative power in that is in them. They are shortchanging themselves of the health and wholeness that God intends for them to have. They are speaking words of death and not life. To put it bluntly, "Our negative words can literally kill us." We must replace negative words about our health with positive words. We should speak words that are in line with the Word of God such as:

31

"By Jesus' stripes I am healed."

"No weapon formed against my body can prosper"

"I am redeemed from the curse of sickness and disease."

"I have a long satisfying life."

"I shall live and not die and declare the works of the Lord."

"My body is the temple of the Holy Spirit. The same Spirit that raised Jesus' body from the dead is making alive my mortal body."

"I am strong in the Lord and the power of His might."

"Everything works in my body according to God's divine purpose."

"I walk in supernatural divine health and wholeness."

When we speak positive words in line with the Word of God over our bodies, we allow the supernatural power of God to manifest health and wholeness in our bodies. When we speak negative words over our bodies, we hinder God from manifesting His will in our lives; and instead, we allow Satan to manifest his agenda. Our words hinder or activate the plans of God or the plans of Satan.

Satan will speak negative thoughts to our minds to see if we will receive them. According to Matthew 6:31, "Take no thought, saying..." We receive a thought by speaking the thought. When we continually speak thoughts from Satan, they will manifest in our lives. Conversely, if we continually speak words in line with the Word of God, God's Word will manifest in our lives.

Sometimes, Satan will put symptoms on you and see what you call them. The Lord gave me this revelation after dealing with a situation concerning my sister. My sister called to tell me that her husband was taking her to the hospital due to some symptoms with her heart. I immediately started to pray and began the drive to the town where my sister lives–which is around a hundred miles away. When I got to the hospital, my sister was in the emergency room. They immediately took her in for examination as they normally do for a person with heart attack symptoms. After the examination they found nothing, and the symptoms disappeared. She was released to go home. The next day I was praising God as I was taking my morning walk. As I praised God, God spoke these words to me, "The devil will put symptoms on you and see what you call them." Many people in the same situation as my sister would have said words like, "I believe I am having a heart attack." The words that we speak establish things in our lives. As I stated earlier, what we truly believe in our heart and confess with our mouth will come to pass in our lives–whether it is good or bad. Our words are powerful, especially when we speak what we truly believe.

When we are hit with a symptom of sickness, we must be careful about the words we speak. According to Luke 6:45, out of the abundance of our heart, our mouth will speak. What is abundantly in your heart? Is there an abundance of God's Word? Or, is there an abundance of words of fear? To speak the right things, right things must be abundantly in our heart. Words are established in our heart by what we meditate on the most. If we meditate on fear-filled words, our heart will be full of fear. If we meditate on the Word of God, our heart will be full of faith. So, when attacks occur, we will speak the words that our heart is filled with. 1 Peter 5:8 says the devil walks around seeking whom he may devour. The devil is watching what we say. If we speak words contrary to God's Word, the devil can establish his will in our lives. Don't allow the devil to use your own words to destroy you.

The Good News Translation (GNT) of Ephesians 4:29 reads, "Do not use harmful words, but only helpful words, the kind that build up and provide what is needed, so that what you say will do good to those who hear you." Don't use words that will harm your health, but use only words that will help, build up and provide what is needed for health and wholeness, so that what you say will do you good. Feed your heart the right things: God's Word. By doing so, you will speak the right words, causing divine health and wholeness to be manifested in your life.

PRAYER:

Father God, thank You for showing me how powerful my words are. Forgive me for any negative words that I have been saying concerning my health. In the Name of Jesus, I bind and cast out anything I have allowed the devil to implement in my life because of the words I have spoken. Help me to speak words that are in line with Your Word which will allow the manifestation of divine health and wholeness in my life. I pray this in Jesus' Name. Amen!

CONFESSION:

I make a commitment to mediate on the Word of God concerning my health and wholeness. By doing so, I will speak the Word of God which will be in abundance in my heart. I will not allow negative words to come out of my mouth concerning my health. I realize there is creative power in my words. Life and death are in my words! So, I choose to speak life which will create the divine health and wholeness that God desires to manifest in my life.

PERSONAL THOUGHTS:

_____

_____

_____

_____

_____

_____

_____

_____

_____

_____

_____

_____

_____

_____

_____

_____

_____

_____

_____

DAY 6

Being Led by The Spirit

Scriptures:

John 16:13 Modern English Version (MEV)–
But when the Spirit of truth comes, ***He will***
guide you into all truth. *For He will not speak*
on His own authority. But He will speak what-
ever He hears, and He will tell you things that
are to come.

John 14:26 Amplified Bible (AMP)–*But the*
Helper (Comforter, Advocate, Intercessor—
Counselor, Strengthener, Standby), the Holy
Spirit, whom the Father will send in My name
[in My place, to represent Me and act on My
behalf], ***He will teach you all things****. And*
He will help you remember everything that I
have told you.

As born-again believers, we are born of the Spirit of God.
God's spirit indwells us. Our bodies are temples of the Holy

Spirit. According to John 14:26, the Holy Spirit is our helper and will teach us all things. John 16:13 tells us that the Holy Spirit will guide us in all truth. The Holy Spirit will guide us in carrying out God's perfect will for our lives; and, it is God's perfect will for us to walk in divine health and wholeness. To do that, we must be led by the Holy Spirit. On our own, we are not smart enough to know all that we need to do, or all that God has done for us to live in divine health and wholeness.

Hosea 4:6 states that God's people are destroyed for lack of knowledge. Many people practice poor health habits because they lack knowledge. People literally destroy their bodies without having any idea that their daily practices are detrimental to their health. Today, so much knowledge is available about developing good health habits. We can read books, watch TV programs, and view website content on promoting good health. Christian doctors and scientists have been inspired by God to teach the Body of Christ things to do to have good health. We must maintain a teachable attitude and be willing to learn so we can benefit from this knowledge.

This wealth of knowledge concerning physical health is powerful. But what is even more powerful than knowledge is wisdom. The Holy Spirit allows us to tap into the very wisdom of God. Wisdom enables us to effectively use knowledge. With so much knowledge available, we need the Holy Spirit to give us wisdom to maneuver through it so we can know what is beneficial to us individually. You are unique; and only the Holy Spirit, who knows your body in minute detail, can direct you to the perfect plan to bring maximum health to your body.

Through the Holy Spirit, you will be able to tailor the available knowledge to meet the needs of your uniquely-made body.

In addition to the natural knowledge available to us, the Holy Spirit will teach us things beyond human knowledge. The Holy Spirit will speak to our born-again spirit, making available to us the wisdom of God and divine revelations. There have been times when the Holy Spirit has directed me to do certain natural things for my health. Later, scientific researchers started saying the same things that the Holy Spirit had already revealed to me.

The Holy Spirit will give you a rhema word, that is, a word from God that is a specific word to you, directing you in a specific situation. Have you ever been buying groceries, when a voice said, "Put back that bag of chips?" Or, while turning into the drive-through lane of a fast food restaurant, a voice in you may say, "Don't stop here?" That voice is the Holy Spirit giving you a rhema word from God, trying to lead you to make better health choices. The Holy Spirit is your teacher and knows all things pertaining to living in divine health and wholeness.

Many of God's people are suffering with illnesses, and even some have prematurely departed because they did not obey God in seemingly trivial things. Some may say they were obedient to God in starting a church, teaching a Bible Study, or feeding the poor; but, they may have been disobedient when the Holy Spirit dealt with them about keeping their hands out of the cookie jar. Proverbs 3:5-6 speaks of trusting in God with all our heart and not leaning to our own understanding, but in *all* our ways acknowledging God so He will direct our paths. God will direct our paths through the Holy Spirit which is within us. Therefore, we should consult with the Holy Spirit in *all* our ways regardless of how insignificant it may seem. God is interested in every minute detail of our lives. We may be expecting the voice of the Holy Spirit to say something like, "Go to Africa and become a missionary." Instead, the Holy Spirit may say, "Walk around the block every day." Many times, it is what we do with those seemingly insignificant directions that will enable us to fulfill God's will for our lives.

To live a long life of divine health and wholeness, seek wisdom from the Holy Spirit. Be open to listening for His voice that is within you; and above all, obey directions from Him regardless of how trivial they may seem to be.

In your pursuit for health and wholeness, remember to ask for help. According to John 14:26, the Holy Spirit is our **Helper**. I believe one of the purest prayers we can pray is the simple prayer, "HELP!" When we pray this prayer, our **Helper** gets involved in our lives, enabling us to tap into the supernatural assistance that is available to us through Him. So, ask for help. Ask the Holy Spirit to **help** you live the life of divine health and wholeness that is promised in God's Word.

Allow the Holy Spirit to teach, guide and help you live a life of health and wholeness that is far beyond the norm.

PRAYER:

Lord, thank You so much for giving to me Your Holy Spirit. I now ask for HELP from the Holy Spirit, who is my helper and teacher, to guide me in living a life of divine health and wholeness. Lord, help me to listen to the voice of the Holy Spirit and to obey the guidance from the Holy Spirit in governing even the minute details of my life. Thank you for the knowledge that You have made available to me and the wisdom to use this knowledge in a way that will best meet the needs of my uniquely-created body. I pray this in Jesus' Name. Amen!

CONFESSION:

I will not be destroyed by the lack of knowledge. I will not neglect my Helper, the Holy Spirit. I will seek guidance from the Holy Spirit to direct me in using knowledge concerning health and wholeness in a way that will best meet the needs of my uniquely-created body. I will listen to and obey the directions from the Holy Spirit regardless how trivial the directions may seem. With the help of the Holy Spirit, I am walking in the divine health and wholeness that God intends for me.

PERSONAL THOUGHTS:

DAY 7

Saying More than Grace over Your Food

Scriptures:

> ***Romans 8:13 (KJV)*** – *For if ye live after the flesh, ye shall die: but if ye through the Spirit do mortify the deeds of the body, ye shall live.*

> ***Galatians 5:16 (KJV)*** – *This I say then, Walk in the Spirit, and ye shall not fulfil the lust of the flesh.*

Many of us from our youth have been saying grace over our food before eating. We *should* pray over our food. We are so blessed to have food to eat. Thanking God for our food is important. Being blessed with food is something we should never take for granted. Also, we do not know what impurities may be in our food; therefore, we should pray for God to bless our food before we eat it.

I also believe that prayer is needed before the food is placed before us. Prayer is needed in selecting the food that we eat. We need to pray and ask God, "What should I eat?" Many times, when deciding what to eat, we ask ourselves, "What do I have a taste for?" What we are really doing is we are asking our flesh, "What are you craving for?" We are setting ourselves up to be led by the flesh and not by the Spirit of God. Many times, the plate that we say grace over is in no way what God would have us to eat. We are making choices based on our own fleshly desires, and then we ask God to bless them. Instead of asking God to bless mess, ask God what we should eat and then thank Him that He has prepared a healthy meal for us to enjoy and benefit from.

When you are grocery shopping, perusing a menu at restaurant or deciding what to prepare for a meal, pray. Ask God for directions in making those decisions. Then, listen to the voice of the Holy Spirit. Those occasions determine whether we will be led by the Spirit or by the flesh.

God will prepare a table for us in the presence of our enemies. Our enemies are anything that is trying to steal, kill and destroy our lives. Sickness and disease are our enemies. When we allow God to prepare our table, it will be a table of good, healthy food that will help destroy our enemies. When we allow our flesh to prepare the table, we may be aiding our enemies in stealing, killing, and destroying our lives.

So, the next time you say grace over your food, let it be over food that was chosen by the Spirit and not the flesh. When the food is chosen by the Spirit, it will be food we can truly be thankful for, and it will bring health and life to our bodies.

PRAYER:

Lord, thank You for the revelation of being led by the Holy Spirit in determining what I should eat. Forgive me for making my own fleshly choices about food and then asking You to bless mess. Lord, help me to be more sensitive to the leading of the Holy Spirit, so that I will make the right choices concerning what I should eat. I pray this in Jesus' Name. Amen!

CONFESSION:

According to Romans 8:13, if I live by the flesh, I will die. If I live by the Spirit, I will live. Therefore, I choose to be led by the Spirit and not by the flesh when it comes to what I should eat. I will not just say grace over my food, but I also will consult the Holy Spirit in deciding what should be placed on the table before me. This will enable me to walk in the health and wholeness that God intends for me.

PERSONAL THOUGHTS:

DAY 8

Exercise

Scripture:

I Timothy 4:8 – *For bodily exercise profiteth little: but godliness is profitable unto all things, having promise of the life that is now is and of that which is to come.*

1 Timothy 4:8 The Voice (VOICE)–*Although training your body has certain payoffs, godliness benefits all things—holding promise for life here and now and promise for the life that is coming.*

When some read 1 Timothy 4:8, they conclude that bodily exercise has little profit, so it is something that can be ignored. However, this scripture is saying that being disciplined in the Word of God to develop godly character is more important than disciplining the body in exercise to develop a fit body. Godly character greatly benefits you now on earth and in eternity. A fit body greatly benefits you while you on earth. Our body is our

47

earth suit. We need it to function here. Once we depart from earth, we will no longer need our earth suit. We will leave our bodies behind. Godly character allows us to do God's work on the earth; and when we depart from here, we take our character with us. I do agree that being disciplined in the Word of God to develop Godly character is more important than being disciplined in exercise to develop a fit body.

According to The Voice Translation of 1 Timothy 4:8, bodily exercise has *certain payoffs*. And those payoffs are important to us while we are on earth. If we are going to impact this world for Christ, we not only need Godly character; but also, we need fit bodies. Physical exercise is vitally important to the well-being of our bodies. God made our bodies with moving parts; and, He made our bodies to move.

I like to compare physical exercise with fasting food. Many times, physical exercise is something that the flesh just does not want to do. Just as fasting food is something the flesh does not want to do. In both cases, we are not to allow the flesh to have its way. When Paul wrote the book of First Timothy, physical exercise was a part of everyday life. Manual labor was necessary in occupations and daily chores for most people. Today, physical exercise is not a built-in part of life in many cases. Many people have to disciple themselves to do it. Since there is benefit in physical exercise, the flesh will fight against it. The flesh would rather lie on the couch and watch TV with a remote control and a bag of potato chips.

We can exercise and pray, just as we would fast and pray. While exercising, it is a perfect time to meditate on the Word of God, pray in the spirit, and listen for the voice of God. Exercising can be a time to build up our bodies as well as build up our relationship with our Father God.

As I stated earlier, God created our bodies to move. When you exercise, praise God for whatever physical activity you are currently able to do, and your physical ability will increase. Don't take the ability to move lightly. It is in God that we live, move, and have our being according to Acts 17:28. So, move your body in physical exercise for the glory of God, and receive all the benefits that bodily exercise has to offer.

PRAYER:

Father God, I praise You that You created my body to move. I praise You for the physical exercise I am able to do. Forgive me if I have taken lightly the opportunity to exercise and keep my body in top physical condition. Lord, help me to be diligent in exercising so that I can be better fit to carry out Your will on earth. I pray this in Jesus' Name. Amen.

CONFESSION:

I will not take lightly the ability to move. I purpose to do physical exercise regularly so I can be more efficient in carrying out God's will on earth. I will use my time of exercise as a time to commune with my Father God and enjoy His presence.

PERSONAL THOUGHTS:

_____

_____

_____

_____

_____

_____

_____

_____

_____

_____

_____

_____

_____

_____

_____

_____

_____

_____

DAY 9

Perfect Weight

Scripture:

Proverbs 11:1 – *A false balance is abomination to the Lord: but a just weight is his delight.*

Deuteronomy 25:15 – *But thou shalt have a perfect and just weight, a perfect and just measure shall thou have: that thy days may be lengthened in the land which the Lord thy God giveth thee.*

For most of my life, weight was something that I battled with from one extreme to another. When I was a little girl around eight years of age, people would point out how skinny I was. I came from a family that thought plump was pretty. My sister was plump and so pretty with her apple cheeks that got pinched a lot. Family members would say to my sister, "Oh, you are so pretty!" and say to me, "You are so skinny." As a young child, I began to be concerned about my weight. I would wish that I were fatter. I began to eat more; and, by the time I was in junior high school, my wish had been granted. Now in my early teens, I was larger than the other girls in my class. As a result, I became very shy and self-conscious. From high school through most of my adult life, I battled with my weight. I went on all kinds of diets and bought a lot of the fitness equipment that advertised on infomercials. I would lose weight, only to gain back more. For many years, weight was consistently on my prayer list. I finally realized that eating well and exercise was the key to my perfect weight. And instead of dieting, I had to establish a lifestyle of eating healthy. I knew I needed God's help because there was no way I could do this on my own. In the process of establishing this lifestyle, I would go to extremes. At one point I had lost so much weight that people would ask me if I were sick. Family members who had not seen me in a while were really concerned about my weight loss; and, I became concerned. It seemed as if the devil was overwhelming me with thoughts like, "What if the weight loss is really a result of sickness?" To add to my fears, I was not feeling very well, and a dear friend had recently died unexpectedly of a rare ailment. I began to fight the fear of being seriously ill. At one point I was battling fear so much that I couldn't sleep. So, one night I just got out of bed with my Bible and began to pray about my weight and health. To my surprise I flipped open my Bible, and my eyes were directed to Proverbs 11:1 which reads, "A false balance is abomination to the Lord: but **a just weight is his delight**." I hadn't ever remembered reading this verse before. In my spirit I knew this was God's Word to me as an answer to prayer. I was off-balance. I had gone to an extreme with this weight loss. I had depleted my body of vital vitamins and minerals; and, that was why I was feeling so poorly. I realized that God delights in a just and balanced weight. God did not want me to go from one extreme to another. I began to confess, "A just weight is God's delight." As I confessed the Word of God, the Holy Spirit started leading me on things to do to get in balance.

I now realize that the perfect weight is not about the way I look, but it is about being healthy. What is a perfect weight for one person may not be the perfect weight for another. The media feeds us images of people who are perceived as having the perfect body, causing us to compare ourselves with these images. We become discontent with ourselves when we make those comparisons. For some of us, it is not meant for us to be a dress size 2 like the model in the magazine; a size 14 may be our perfect size. God knows the perfect weight for each of us. He is our Creator, our manufacturer. He made us completely unique. It is unwise to compare yourself with others, according to II Corinthians 10:12. This scripture in the Amplified Bible reads, "Not that we [have the audacity to] venture to class or [even to] compare ourselves with some who exalt and furnish testimonials for themselves! However, when they measure themselves with themselves and compare themselves with one another, they are without understanding and behave unwisely." When we compare ourselves with others, we don't understand that God created us as unique individuals; and, we begin to behave unwisely, trying to be like someone other than ourselves.

God knows your perfect weight. Allow the Holy Spirit to lead you to that perfect weight by guiding you in the healthy lifestyle that God has ordained for you personally.

Consider God's promise from Deuteronomy 25:15 – *"But thou shalt have a **perfect and just weight**, a perfect and just measure shall thou have: **that thy days may be lengthened** in the land which the Lord thy God giveth thee."* Receive, believe, and confess this promise from God and you shall have the perfect weight that God ordained just for you, and you will live a long, divine, healthy life.

PRAYER:

Father God, I thank You that You know me very well. Forgive me if I have been comparing myself with others or have only been concerned about my looks. As my Creator, You know my perfect weight. Lord, help me to reach and maintain the perfect weight that You have for me, so that I can live the long, divine, healthy life that will glorify You. I pray this in Jesus' Name. Amen.

CONFESSION:

A just weight is God's delight. I have the perfect and just weight that my Creator has ordained for me, so that my days may be lengthened to do all that God has for me to do.

PERSONAL THOUGHTS:

DAY 10

Rest

Scriptures:

Proverbs 3:24 (VOICE)–*Your mind will be clear, free from fear; when you lie down to rest, you will be refreshed by sweet sleep.*

Hebrews 4:9-11 The Passion Translation (TPT)–*So we conclude that there is still a full and complete "rest" waiting for believers to experience. ¹⁰ As we enter into God's faith-rest life we cease from our own works, just as God celebrates his finished works and rests in them. ¹¹ So then we must give our all and be eager to experience this faith-rest life, so that no one falls short by following the same pattern of doubt and unbelief.*

John 5:19 Contemporary English Version (CEV)–*Jesus told the people: I tell you for certain that the Son cannot do anything on his own.*

He can do only what he sees the Father doing,
and he does exactly what he sees the Father do.

Rest is vitally important to our health and wholeness. Rest refreshes and restores our bodies and promotes the natural healing processes that God has built into our bodies. According to Hebrews 4:9-11, there is a rest that God has prepared for His children. God promises in Proverbs 3:24 that when we lie down to rest, we will be refreshed by sweet sleep. But why isn't this always happening in the lives of believers?

We all have paid the price for not getting enough rest. This lack of rest can be caused by having too much activity in our lives, whether it is physical or mental activity. Physically, we can burn the candle at both ends by having too many demands on our lives. Many times, when our bodies are tired and we are in bed, our minds continue to work, trying to figure out solutions to our problems. Have you ever been in a nice, comfortable bed trying to go to sleep, and rest seems to escape you? Thoughts are running through your mind like bullets. As you mentally rehearse and evaluate your busy day, all the things that you should have done or should not have done run through your mind. After running through the "should-not-have-dones" and "should-have-dones" come the "what-ifs." You start thinking, "What if this or that happens because of what I did and should not have done, or because of what I should have done and didn't do?" Now, you are muddling through thoughts like, "How do I solve the 'what-if' problems that may occur because of the things I should have done, or things I should not have done?"

The next thing you know, it is morning and the rehearsal of the previous day's activities has taken up the entire night. Needless to say, you are not in the best physical or mental condition to face a new day.

When scenarios like this occur in our lives, we can see that we are not living the faith-rest life described in Hebrews 4:9-11. You see, before becoming born-again believers, we were conditioned to make our own plans and to take care of our own problems. As born-again believers, we must realize that we are no longer on our own when it comes to making plans and solving problems. We now have a relationship with our Father God, and He has given us His Spirit to guide us. According to Hebrews 4:10, to have a faith-rest life, we must cease from our own works. Ceasing from our own works does not mean we do nothing. It means that, instead of being busy doing our own agenda, we follow God's agenda for our lives. God has the perfect plan for us, and He has everything already figured out. God has already solved every problem we might encounter in life. So, rather than toiling trying to come up with our own plans and solving our own problems, we can just get instructions from our omniscient Father God and do whatever He tells us to do. This is how Jesus lived His life. According to John 5:19, Jesus did nothing on His own. Jesus had ceased from his own works and only did what the Father showed him to do. Jesus lived the faith-rest life.

Hebrews 4:10 tells us that if we have doubt and unbelief, we cannot enter the rest that God has for us. To enjoy that rest, we must totally put our faith in Him by ceasing from our own works and surrendering to His plan for our lives. We will live the faith-rest life when we do only those things that God has prescribed for us.

So, the next time you are trying to sleep and your mind is flooded by thoughts of "should-have-dones," "should-not-have-dones," and "what-ifs", cease from your own works and surrender all to God. Then, you will experience the promise found in Proverbs 3:24 – *Your mind will be clear, free from fear; when you lie down to rest, you will be refreshed by sweet sleep.* You will experience the health and wholeness that comes with living the faith-rest life.

PRAYER:

Father God, thank You for providing rest for my weary soul and body. Forgive me for toiling with my own agenda and problems in life. Thank You for revealing to me that I can trade in my agenda for Your agenda by ceasing from my own works and surrendering my life totally to You. As I do this, Your rest is coming out of my inner-most being and is impacting my soul and body. Now Holy Spirit, help me to live the faith-rest life. Thank You that I will walk in health and wholeness because of the faith-rest life that You have provided for me!

I pray this in Jesus' Name. Amen!

CONFESSION:

I choose to live the faith-rest life. I cease from my own works, that is, working to bring about my own agenda and solving my own problems. I put away doubt, fear and unbelief which comes with following my own agenda. Father God, I trade in my agenda for Your agenda by surrendering my life to You. I will only do those things that You show me to do. I am enjoying the rest that You have provided for me. Now, my mind is clear, free from fear; when I lie down to rest, I will be refreshed by sweet sleep. I am experiencing the benefits that rest brings to my mind and body.

PERSONAL THOUGHTS:

_____

_____

_____

_____

_____

_____

_____

_____

_____

_____

_____

_____

_____

_____

_____

_____

_____

_____

DAY 11

Walking in Your Divine Purpose Brings Health and Wholeness

Scriptures:

John 4:27-34 (NKJV)

31 In the meantime His disciples urged Him, saying, "Rabbi, eat."

32 But He said to them, "I have food to eat of which you do not know."

33 Therefore the disciples said to one another, "Has anyone brought Him anything to eat?"

34 Jesus said to them, "My food is to do the will of Him who sent Me, and to finish His work."

In John 4, Jesus was tired, hungry, and thirsty from traveling. The disciples went into the city to get food for Him. In the meantime, Jesus ministered to the Samaritan woman and many other people of Samaria. By the time the disciples got back with food, Jesus was already physically energized to the point that the disciples asked, "Has anyone brought Jesus anything to eat?" Jesus pointed out that He had gained physical strength by *doing the will of His Father and by pursuing His divine purpose.*

There is energy and strength in fulfilling God's purpose for your life. When we step out and do the will of God, supernatural health and strength kicks in. We begin to operate in health and strength that is beyond the natural. God causes His "super" to be put on our natural. The key to tapping into this supernatural energy is living our lives fulfilling our divine purpose. Each person has a God-given purpose. Once we find that purpose and pursue it with all our heart, we will tap into an amazing strength that energizes our physical bodies.

We are three-part beings – spirit, soul, and body. As a born-again believer, our spirit is already in line with the will of God for our life. Our soul is made up of our mind, will, and emotions. Many times, on the soulish level, we may have our own agenda for our life which may be contrary to the will of God. When we fight against God's will for our life, it is detrimental to our health and wholeness because while our born-again spirit is aligned with God's will, our soul contradicts the will of God. This disagreement between the soul and the spirit causes stress on the body, resulting in illness. To eliminate this disagreement, we must renew our mind on the Word of God. This allows our soul to get in line with the will of God. Once our spirit and soul are in alignment with the will of God, then our body will also line up. When we are pursuing the divine will of God for our life, our spirit, soul, and body are in harmony, thus producing the abundant life that God intends for us to have. Also, our joy will be full, giving strength and energy to our body. We know this because Nehemiah 8:10 states that the joy of the Lord is our strength.

Our divine purpose will never be a selfish desire, but it will always be about meeting the needs of others. As Jesus got caught up in meeting the needs of the Samaritan people, all His physical needs were met. He was no longer tired, hungry, or thirsty. When we are in our divine purpose, we are a great blessing to others. As we bless others, our lives become even more blessed. We will have joy and peace that will bring health and wholeness to our lives. As we get excited about doing the will of God and fulfilling His divine purpose for our lives, then just like Jesus, we will be supernaturally energized, and our health and strength will be renewed.

I believe the happiest and most fulfilled people are those who are fulfilling their God-given purpose. So, stop fighting against your divine purpose! Flow with God and experience health and wholeness that is beyond the natural.

PRAYER:

Father God, thank You so much that You have a divine purpose for my life. Lead me into my purpose. Forgive me if I have been pursuing other things rather than Your will for my life. Help me to lay aside all other agendas and pursue Your divine purpose.

I pray this in Jesus' Name. Amen.

CONFESSION:

I will lay aside selfish agendas in my life. I will pursue God's divine will for my life. In doing so, I will live a fulfilled life that will be a blessing to others. As I pursue God's purpose for my life, my body will be supernaturally energized, and I will walk in the divine health and wholeness that my Father God intends for me.

PERSONAL THOUGHTS:

_____

_____

_____

_____

_____

_____

_____

_____

_____

_____

_____

_____

_____

_____

_____

_____

_____

_____

_____

_____

DAY 12

A Long Satisfying Life

Scriptures:

Psalm 91:14-16 Amplified Bible (AMP)–[14]
Because he set his love on Me, therefore I will
save him; I will set him [securely] on high,
because he knows My name [he confidently
trusts and relies on Me, knowing I will never
abandon him, no, never]. [15] He will call upon
Me, and I will answer him; I will be with him
in trouble; I will rescue him and honor him. [16]
*"With **a long life I will satisfy him;** And I will let*
him see My salvation.

Proverbs 3:1-2 New Living Translation (NLT)–
My child, never forget the things I have taught
you. Store my commands in your heart. [2] If you
*do this, **you will live many years, and your life***
will be satisfying.

Proverbs 3:1-2 Amplified Bible (AMP)–*My son, do not forget my teaching, But let your heart keep my commandments; ² For length of days and years of life [worth living] And tranquility and prosperity [the wholeness of life's blessings] they will add to you.*

We can see in God's Word that He has promised long life to those who trust Him. Long life will not be such a great reward if we have a long life filled with suffering, turmoil, and lack. According to Psalm 91:16 and Proverbs 3:2, God has promised that our lives will be satisfying years worth living and filled with tranquility and prosperity. Isn't this awesome! A satisfying, long life is a part of walking in divine health and wholeness.

In Exodus chapter 12, we see how the blood of a lamb with no blemishes was applied to the door post of the houses of the Children of Israel to prevent premature deaths in their homes. Verse 23 in the New Life Version (NLV) reads, "when He sees the blood around the door, the Lord will pass over the door. He will not let the one who destroys come into your houses to kill you." The blood of the unblemished lamb was a foreshadowing of the Blood of Jesus. Just like the blood of the lamb in Exodus chapter 12 prevented premature death, so does Jesus' Blood. His Blood will not allow the one who destroys to take you out prematurely. If you have been in certain churches, you may have heard the older saints say, "I plead the Blood of Jesus." They are applying the Blood of Jesus against the destroyer of life. So, when faced with a life-threatening situation, plead the Blood of Jesus. This will stop the destroyer in his tracks.

God has promised you a long, satisfying life of divine health and wholeness. Believe it! Receive it! Don't settle for less! When situations occur that are contrary to God's promise, PLEAD THE BLOOD OF JESUS. This will STOP the destroyer from causing premature death in your life.

PRAYER:

Thank You, Father God, for showing me the power that I have in the Blood of Jesus. By the Blood of Jesus, I can STOP the destroyer in my life. Lord, help me to make full use of the Blood of Jesus. Thank you for a long satisfying life.

I pray this in Jesus' Name. Amen!

CONFESSION:

I PLEAD THE BLOOD OF JESUS over my life. The destroyer is STOPPED in my life. I will not die prematurely. I have a long, satisfying life of divine health and wholeness filled with tranquility and prosperity.

PERSONAL THOUGHTS:

_____

_____

_____

_____

_____

_____

_____

_____

_____

_____

_____

_____

_____

_____

_____

_____

_____

_____

_____

_____

In the Fight for Health and Wholeness

Romans 8:37

The Passion Translation (TPT)

Yet even in the midst of all these things, we triumph over them all, for God has made us to be more than conquerors, and his demonstrated love is our glorious victory over everything!

DAY 13

Keep Your Foot on the Faith Pedal

Scriptures:

Luke 18:1, 8 (AMP)

Also [Jesus] told them a parable to the effect that they ought always to pray and not to turn coward (faint, lose heart, and give up).

I tell you, He will defend and protect and avenge them speedily. However, will He find [persistence in] faith in the earth?

We know that by grace, God has already provided everything we need in life. And we know that it takes faith to receive everything that is already done by grace. But the question is: "Why does it sometimes seem to take so long for what is already done in grace to manifest in the natural?"

I know of many born-again believers who have not seen the manifestation of what they have been praying for. And they have been waiting for what seems to be a long time for the manifestation. Also, I know if there is any short-coming, it is in us and not in God. Therefore, I am seeking an answer to this question, so we will know where we are coming up short.

Let's look at the words of Jesus in Luke 18:1, 8, to shine light on the answer to this question.

Luke 18:1, 8 (AMP)

Also [Jesus] told them a parable to the effect that they ought always to pray and not to turn coward (faint, lose heart, and give up).

*I tell you, He [God] will defend and protect and avenge them **speedily**. However, will He find [**persistence** in] faith in the earth?*

I have bolded the word "speedily". Jesus is telling us that God intends for the manifestation of our prayers to come speedily. But why aren't we seeing this?

When we think about speed, we may relate it to a car speeding down a highway headed toward a destination. As we keep our foot on the gas pedal, we are getting closer and closer to our destination. But if we take our foot off the gas pedal, we are no longer moving forward. Let's look at the gas pedal as the faith pedal. As long as we stay on the faith pedal, we are moving forward and getting closer and closer to the manifestation of the answer to our prayer. We are on the faith pedal as long as we are focusing on God's Word pertaining to the problem, mediating on that word day and night, diligently expecting the God-promised outcome and praising God for the manifestation. But if we allow doubt, fear, unbelief, or discouragement to cause us to take our spiritual foot off the faith pedal, we will faint, lose heart, and give up on reaching our destination. Many times, once we have fainted and given up, we regroup by getting back in the Word of God and getting our foot back on the faith pedal. So again, we are moving forward to our destination, but we have delayed our arrival time. What will determine how fast we will get to our destination or if we arrive there at all, is how *persistent* we are about keeping our foot on the faith pedal.

For example, you are standing in faith for the healing of your body. You know what God's Word says concerning healing. You know that by Jesus' stripes, you are healed. You know your body is the temple of the Holy Spirit, and the same Spirit that raised Jesus' body from the dead is in you, quickening your mortal body. You know God sent His Word to heal. You know that no weapon formed against you can prosper. But in the face of a negative diagnosis or symptom, you are gripped with fear and begin to doubt God's Word concerning healing. At this point, your foot is off the faith pedal, and you are no longer moving towards the manifestation of the answer to your prayer. Instead, you begin to faint and lose heart. How long you stay in this state of fear, doubt and unbelief will delay, or even forfeit, the manifestation of the answer to your prayer. But if, on the other hand, in the face of a negative diagnosis or symptoms, you are persistent and consistent on your stand in faith–that is, you refuse to waver on your belief that God's Word is the absolute truth–then, your foot remains on the faith pedal, and you are speedily moving towards the manifestation of your healed body. God's Word will manifest in your life speedily when you have persistent, consistent, uninterrupted faith.

Check yourself regularly to make sure you are still on the faith pedal. Here are some symptoms of not being on the faith pedal. These should set off a FAITH ALARM so that you will immediately get back on the faith pedal:

- You are talking about the problem more than you are talking about the Word of God that applies to the problem. **Be Alarmed! You are OFF the faith pedal!**
- You are focusing on words, symptoms, and circumstances which are contrary to the Word of God rather than focusing on the Word of God. **Be Alarmed! You are OFF the faith pedal!**
- You have stop praising God. **Be Alarmed! You are OFF the faith pedal!**
- You are angry that the manifestation has not come. **Be Alarmed! You are OFF the faith pedal!**
- You are anxious and worried. **Be Alarmed! You are OFF the faith pedal!**
- You are whining and complaining. **Be Alarmed! You are OFF the faith pedal!**
- You are crying and begging. **Be Alarmed! You are OFF the faith pedal!**

- You are discouraged. **Be Alarmed! You are OFF the faith pedal!**
- You are fearful. **Be Alarmed! You are OFF the faith pedal!**
- You are doubting God's Word and faithfulness. **Be Alarmed! You are OFF the faith pedal!**
- You have lost your joy. **Be Alarmed! You are OFF the faith pedal!**
- You have lost hope. **Be Alarmed! You are OFF the faith pedal!**

The longer the enemy can keep you off the faith pedal, the more delayed the manifestation will be. Make the commitment when you first pray about the problem that no matter how long it takes, you are not going to get off the faith pedal. Sometimes, there may be multiple attacks against you, and it may seem you are in an uphill battle. In these times, you may have to push your faith pedal to the floor. Yes, I said, "FLOOR IT!" You can't afford to take your foot off the pedal when you are in an uphill battle because you will not only stop making progress, but also, you will roll back and lose ground that has already been taken. In times like these, increase your time in the Word of God, get loud with your praise, speak the Word of God only and become even more determined to stay on the faith pedal!

The question to you is, "**Will God find that you are persistent in your faith?**" That is, will God find that you are persistently keeping pressure on the faith pedal? If so, you are working with God and causing the answer to your prayer to be manifested *speedily*.

PRAYER:

Father God, help me to stay persistent in my faith so that I will not hinder or delay the manifestation of what You have promised. Help me to not to fall prey to doubt, fear and unbelief which are hinderances to the manifestation of Your promises. Help me to recognize when my spiritual foot is no longer on the faith pedal, so I can immediately get back on the pedal. I praise You that You have already provided everything I need, and You have shown me how to receive the manifestation by keeping pressure on the faith pedal.

I pray this in Jesus' Name. Amen!

CONFESSION:

Right now, I commit to keeping my spiritual foot on the faith pedal–no matter what. I will not delay or stop the manifestation of what God has promised by taking my spiritual foot off the faith pedal. I will keep pressure on the pedal until I see the full manifestation of what my Father God has promised me through His Word.

PERSONAL THOUGHTS:

_____

_____

_____

_____

_____

_____

_____

_____

_____

_____

_____

_____

_____

_____

_____

_____

_____

_____

_____

DAY 14

Fearless in the Face of Bad Reports

Scriptures:

> *Psalm 112:7 King James Version (KJV)*–*He shall not be afraid of evil tidings: his heart is fixed, trusting in the Lord.*

> *Psalm 112:7 Good News Translation (GNT)*– *He is not afraid of receiving bad news; his faith is strong, and he trusts in the Lord.*

When you are in good health and feeling well is not the time to neglect maintaining and building your faith for divine health and wholeness. Keep the Word of God concerning your health before your eyes and in your meditation every day. Don't allow your faith to dwindle; instead, increase in faith every day.

Many believers wait until their bodies are under attack before they start trying to build their faith concerning healing and wholeness. If you wait until you get a bad report from the doctor to build your faith, fear may get the upper hand. To walk in the supernatural power of God, your faith must be stronger than any fear that may try to overtake you.

I believe that one of the main reasons many believers are defeated by sickness and disease is they spend more of their daily time feeding their fears than they do feeding their faith. Many spend much of their daily time watching TV, engaging in the internet, and interacting in conversations that build fear. Have you noticed how many TV commercials focus on all kinds of dreaded diseases and the side effects of the medications that treat these diseases? Or, how the news media uses statistics to predict doom and gloom about how many will get the flu, or how certain groups of people are prone to certain diseases? If that isn't enough to build fear, there are people who major in conversations about the hopelessness of their sickness and the sicknesses of others. Have you noticed the overwhelming amount of opportunities there are in a day to build fear? As a result, when people's bodies are under attack, their faith is feeble, and their fear is strong. Therefore, we MUST make a conscious effort to feed daily on God's Word concerning our health and wholeness. This is the only way to build strong faith. According to Psalms 112:7, you will not be afraid when you get a bad report because your faith is strong, and your heart is fixed, trusting in God. When you have taken the time to build your trust in God's Word, in the face of a bad doctor's report, you can say from the depths of your heart, "I REFUSE TO FEAR." With strong faith, your heart will not be overtaken by fear and you will walk in the health and wholeness that God has promised in His Word.

PRAYER:

Father God, forgive me if I have been using my daily time building fear rather than building my faith. Help me to increase my faith daily by focusing on Your Word. I thank You, Lord, that You have provided Your Word concerning health and wholeness so that during times of bad health reports, my faith will be strong and unshakeable.

I pray this in Jesus' Name, Amen!

CONFESSION:

I commit to making a conscious effort to meditate daily on God's Word concerning health and wholeness. Therefore, my faith is strong, and I REFUSE TO FEAR in the face of a bad health report because my heart is fixed, trusting in God.

PERSONAL THOUGHTS:

_____

_____

_____

_____

_____

_____

_____

_____

_____

_____

_____

_____

_____

_____

_____

_____

_____

_____

_____

DAY 15

Praise Your Way into Perpetual Health and Wholeness

Scriptures:

> *Psalm 34:1 King James Version (KJV)–I will bless the Lord at all times: his praise shall continually be in my mouth.*

> *Psalm 69:30 Good News Translation (GNT)–I will praise God with a song; I will proclaim his greatness by giving him thanks.*

> *Psalm 106:1 King James Version (KJV)–Praise ye the Lord, O give thanks unto the Lord; for he is good: for his mercy endureth for ever.*

> *Isaiah 25:1 Good News Translation (GNT)– Lord, you are my God; I will honor you and praise your name. You have done amazing things; you have faithfully carried out the plans you made long ago.*

Deuteronomy 10:21 Good News Translation (GNT)–*Praise him—he is your God, and you have seen with your own eyes the great and astounding things that he has done for you.*

Psalm 103:1-5 New Living Translation (NLT)
¹ Let all that I am praise the Lord;
with my whole heart, I will praise his holy name.
² Let all that I am praise the Lord;
may I never forget the good things he does for me.
³ He forgives all my sins
and heals all my diseases.
⁴ He redeems me from death
and crowns me with love and tender mercies.
⁵ He fills my life with good things.
My youth is renewed like the eagle's!

Proverbs 17:22 Good News Translation (GNT)–*Being cheerful keeps you healthy. It is slow death to be gloomy all the time.*

Do you know that you can praise your way into perpetual health and wholeness? Praising is the act of being thankful. When you praise God, you are expressing your trust in Him. You are recognizing God's greatness and His ability to handle any of life's problems. You are casting down fears and anxieties, causing your emotions and body to be at rest. You may start out praising God by reading praise scriptures, listening to or singing praise and worship songs, vocalizing your love for Him, acknowledging His love for you, recognizing God's goodness and faithfulness that has manifested in your life and acknowledging His promises. This may start out as a forced activity, but longer you do it, your born-again spirit becomes involved. You will get to the point that the praise is actually coming out of your spirit, and not just from your mind and emotions. At times you may need to praise in the spirit (in your prayer language) because you just don't have the words to express your gratitude. As praise continues to come from your spirit, your praise will become worship; and, you will experience true peace and joy. You will become cheerful and any gloominess will have to leave.

There are three areas we give praise to God–we praise Him for who He is, we praise Him for what has manifested in our lives, and we praise Him for what will surely manifest based on His promises.

The first area of praise is praising God for who He is. According to Psalm 69:30, we are recognizing God's greatness–that is, His superiority in power, wisdom and might. We praise Him for His character. His goodness, mercy, faithfulness, integrity, kindness, and love. We praise Him for being our Father and our God, and the Creator of heaven and earth. We just praise Him for who He is!

The second area of praise is praising God for the things that He has manifested in our lives. Deuteronomy 10:21 (GNT) reads, *"Praise him—he is your God, and you have seen with your own eyes the great and astounding things that he has done for you."* This is where it gets personal. Think about your personal life and praise God for the astounding things He has done right before your very eyes. Look at your life and remember the times God has protected, provided, healed, and made ways out of no ways, worked miracles, cleaned up messes you made, gave you a second, third, and a fourth chance. Thank Him for His benefits: He forgave your sins, He healed your diseases, He redeemed your very life from destruction, and He surrounded you with His tender mercies and loving kindness! Thank Jesus for His redemptive work that He accomplished over 2,000 years ago. Jesus shed His blood for the remission of your sins, and He took stripes on His body for the healing of *your* body.

The third area of praise is praising God for the things that He has promised, but you have not yet seen manifest in your life. This is where faith is vital. Faith is the evidence of things not yet seen (Hebrews 11:1). Faith stands on the premise that what God has promised will surely come to past. The Bible tells us in Numbers 23:19, New Life Version (NLV) that, *"God is not a man, that He should lie. He is not a son of man, that He should be sorry for what He has said. Has He said, and will He not do it? Has He spoken, and will He not keep His Word?"* Therefore, you can rest assured, fully persuaded that God will carry out whatever He has promised. You don't have to wait to see it to give praise to God. If you truly believe His Word, you can praise God when you see no evidence in the natural realm that what He has promised is coming to pass. You are just simply walking by faith in God's Word and not by what you can see. If you are truly standing in faith, you will celebrate before the manifestation, that is, you will praise God with the same gusto as if it has already been manifested with physical evidence. By praising, you are strengthening your faith and abolishing fear, doubt, and unbelief. Make your only thoughts concerning a promise from God that has yet to be manifested, be thoughts of praise.

For instance, if you are standing in faith for the healing of your body which has yet to manifest, praise God for who He is, praise God for healings and health that are manifested, and praise God for the manifestation of what is not yet seen. In praising God for who He is, you might say, "God, thank you for being my loving Father, the creator of heaven and earth. You are mighty and there is none greater than You. With You all things are possible. Your Word is the ultimate truth. Thank you for Your faithfulness to Your promises." Instead of putting all the focus on healing that has not manifested, spend time praising God for the health and prior healings that already are manifested in your body. Praise God for what is working right in your body, whatever it might be. Don't take the health that is manifested for granted. Maybe you have pains in your left foot, but your right foot is working fine. Praise God for the health you have in your right foot. Now, praise God for the healing that is yet to be manifested based on what God has promised in His Word. God has promised that by the stripes Jesus took on His physical body, your physical body is healed. God is faithful to what He promised. Therefore, your body is healed, and the physical manifestation of the healing will surely come to pass. Now, praise God with the same exuberance as if it has already been physically manifested. So, get your praise on because God is faithful!

Set an atmosphere of praise in your home and everywhere you go. Praise is the perfect antidote for an atmosphere filled with griping, complaining and ungratefulness. Praise changes the atmosphere. Praise changes hopelessness to expectation, sadness to joy, discouragement to encouragement, chaos to peace, pessimism to optimism, weariness to energy, and gloominess to laughter and dancing!

Make praise a lifestyle by allowing praise to continually come out of your mouth. Continual praise produces a cheerful, optimistic attitude. According to Proverbs 17:22 (GNT), a cheerful attitude keeps you healthy and a gloomy attitude will lead you to slow death. So, praise God continually and watch your health improve. By making praise a lifestyle, you will praise your way into divine health and wholeness.

PRAYER:

Lord, I just praise You because You are so great and mighty, and Your words are true. I praise You because I know that every good thing in my life comes from You. I praise You because You are my savior, protector, provider, healer, and a very present help in the time of trouble. Thank You for loving me and taking such good care of me. Help me to make praising You a lifestyle so that I will have a cheerful attitude that will bring health to my body.

I pray this in Jesus' Name. Amen.

CONFESSION:

I will bless the LORD at all times, and I will continually let His praises come out of my mouth. I will develop a lifestyle of praise that causes me to have a cheerful attitude which will bring perpetual health and wholeness to my body.

PERSONAL THOUGHTS:

Enemies of Divine Health and Wholeness

2 Corinthians 2:11

GOD'S WORD Translation (GW)

I don't want Satan to outwit us. After all, we are not igno-rant about Satan's scheming.

DAY 16

Stress

Scriptures:

1 John 4:18–*There is no fear in love; but perfect love casteth out fear: because fear hath torment. He that feareth is not made perfect in love.*

2 Timothy 1:7 King James Version (KJV)–*For God hath not given us the spirit of fear; but of power, and of love, and of a sound mind.*

Sometimes, it may seem as if you have the weight of the world on you. Pressures may be coming from every direction. Your emotions may be like a roller-coaster. You are stressed! Your body is tense, restless, and uneasy. Being in this stressful state is a detriment to your health and wholeness.

Fear is the foundation for all stress. Before the fall of man, Adam and Eve had never experienced fear. They lived in a stress-free environment and didn't have a care in the world. Can you imagine, having never experienced fear? After the Fall, the first knowledge of evil that mankind acquired was the knowledge of fear. It was the immediate result of man's broken relationship with God. According to Genesis 3, after Adam and Eve disobeyed God, they became afraid of God and tried to hide from Him. As a result of their disobedience, they were separated from God spiritually and entered a relationship with Satan, who is the "spirit of fear". When man's spirit became separated from God, fear began to manifest in the soul and body as **stress**. I believe *stress is fear's torment* spoken of in 1 John 4:18. A stressed-filled life is a tormented life.

As a result of the fall of man, stress is a weight or burden that is on people in this world. It is a weight that starts dominating our lives from birth. It was not God's plan for man to be burdened with stress. We now deal with stress resulting from a broken relationship with God, which leads to broken relationships with others. Our broken relationship with God causes stress to manifest as **worry**. Our broken relationship with people causes stress to manifest as **unforgiveness**. So, the two major ways that stress is manifested in our soul and body are through **worry** and **unforgiveness**.

As born-again believers, we must see fear for it really is. It is a sin to fear. "Fear not" may not be explicitly listed as one of the Ten Commandments, but 365 times in the Bible, God has commanded us to fear not. God knew if we succumbed to fear, we would experience stress; and, stress hinders the abundant life that God intends for us to have.

The Cure for Stress

As we stated earlier, fear is the foundation for stress. The cure for stress is found in 1 John 4:18 (KJV):

> *There is no fear in love; but perfect love casteth out fear: because fear hath torment. He that feareth is not made perfect in love.*

Perfect love is the cure! **Perfect love casts out fear.** So, now the question is – How do we get "perfect love"? We get perfect love by getting connected to God who is Perfect Love. If we believe in our heart and confess with our mouth that God loved us so much that He gave His son Jesus to pay the price for the forgiveness our sin, we are no longer separated from God. We are born again into a loving father-child relationship with God as our Father. Our spirit is recreated, and we now have the attributes of our Father God. God not only loves us, but we now have His loving nature as a part of our new nature. As a result of receiving **God's love for us**, we have **God's love in us**. Receiving **God's love for us** takes away the stress of worry; and, **God's love in us** equips us to deal with the stress of unforgiveness. With God's love in us, we can love and forgive others. As we build our relationship with God and grow in revelation of His perfect love for us, our trust in God will grow. As our trust in God grows, our peace increases, and worry diminishes. As we build our relationship with God, the attribute of love, which we inherited from our Father God, will manifest in our relationships with others, causing unforgiveness to be broken off our lives.

According to 2 Timothy 1:7, fear is not from God. Therefore, the torment of fear–stress–is not from God. But God has given us power, love, and a sound mind. We have power within us to overcome stress. We have God's perfect love to cast out fear. And we have a sound mind that is filled with the peace of God. As born-again believers, we are fully equipped to live a stress-free lifestyle.

This chapter, "Stress," has really hit the core of something that God wants His people to know. Therefore, I will elaborate more on the stress of worry and the stress of unforgiveness in the following two chapters. I believe worry and unforgiveness may be the major doors that we, God's people, are allowing the devil to enter through into our lives. Could It be that these are the sins keeping God's people from walking in the health and wholeness that God has promised to His people in His Word? Many times, Christians feel good about themselves when they are not committing the sins of fornication, adultery, lying and stealing. Yet, some commit the sins of worry and unforgiveness as a way of life. Therefore, they are burdened with stress just like the people of the world. Could these be the open doors in the lives of God's people allowing every evil work of the enemy to enter? Could this be at the core of what is causing God's people to be burdened with sickness and disease? We must get real with ourselves and judge ourselves to see if these areas are hindering us from walking in the health and wholeness that God promised. We have been redeemed from the curse of sickness and disease by the stripes of Jesus. NOW, it is time to walk into everything that God has provided for us through the redemptive work of Jesus.

PRAYER:

Help me Lord, to see myself. Show me any area of my life that I have allowed stress to enter. Lord, forgive me for the sin of worry and the sin of unforgiveness. I cast all my care on You because You love and care for me. I now pray in the Spirit over the situations that would try to tempt me to worry or to walk in unforgiveness. When I pray in the Spirit, I am allowing the Holy Spirit to speak Your perfect will through me for these situations. Thank You, Lord, for loving me, forgiving me, and for removing stress from my life. I pray this in Jesus' Name. Amen!

CONFESSION:

I realize that stress adds torment to my life. I make a quality decision to resist the stress of worry and the stress of unforgiveness. Because of God's perfect love for me, I trust Him, and I worry for nothing. God has equipped me with the ability to love and forgive others. So, I choose to forgive by God's perfect love which is in me. I choose not to worry by building my trust in God through His Word. I live a stress-free life which promotes the health and wholeness that my Father God intends for me.

PERSONAL THOUGHTS:

DAY 17

Worry

Scripture:

Proverbs 3:5-8 The Passion Translation (TPT)

[5] Trust in the Lord completely, and do not rely on your own opinions. With all your heart rely on him to guide you, and he will lead you in every decision you make.

[6] Become intimate with him in whatever you do, and he will lead you wherever you go.

[7] Don't think for a moment that you know it all, for wisdom comes when you adore him with undivided devotion and avoid everything that's wrong.

[8] Then you will find the healing refreshment your body and spirit long for.

Philippians 4:6,7 Living Bible (TLB)–[6] *Don't worry about anything; instead, pray about everything; tell God your needs, and don't forget to thank him for his answers.* [7] *If you do this, you will experience God's peace, which is far more wonderful than the human mind can understand. His peace will keep your thoughts and your hearts quiet and at rest as you trust in Christ Jesus.*

John 14:27 (KJV)–[27] *Peace I leave with you, my peace I give unto you: not as the world giveth, give I unto you. Let not your heart be troubled, neither let it be afraid.*

Isaiah 26:3 (KJV)–*Thou wilt keep him in perfect peace, whose mind is stayed on thee: because he trusteth in thee.*

1 Peter 5:7 (KJV)–[7] *Casting all your care upon him; for he careth for you.*

Psalm 46:10 (KJV)–[10] *Be still, and know that I am God...*

Matthew 6:25-33 New English Translation (NET Bible)–[25] *"Therefore I tell you, do not worry about your life, what you will eat or drink,*

*or about your body, what you will wear. Isn't
there more to life than food and more to the body
than clothing? [26] Look at the birds in the sky:
They do not sow, or reap, or gather into barns,
yet your heavenly Father feeds them. Aren't you
more valuable than they are? [27] And which of
you by worrying can add even one hour to his
life? [28] Why do you worry about clothing? Think
about how the flowers of the field grow; they do
not work or spin. [29] Yet I tell you that not even
Solomon in all his glory was clothed like one
of these! [30] And if this is how God clothes the
wild grass, which is here today and tomorrow
is tossed into the fire to heat the oven, won't
he clothe you even more, you people of little
faith? [31] So then, don't worry saying, 'What
will we eat?' or 'What will we drink?' or 'What
will we wear?' [32] For the unconverted pursue
these things, and your heavenly Father knows
that you need them. [33] But above all pursue his
kingdom and righteousness, and all these things
will be given to you as well.*

Trusting God is vital to our walking in the health and wholeness that God has promised us in His Word.

Adam and Eve disobeyed God by trusting in the words
of Satan over the words God had spoken to them concerning
eating from the tree of the knowledge of good and evil. When

man disobeyed God by distrusting Him, the weight of the world came upon him in the form of worry. **Worry is simply the lack of trust in God.** Now, instead of trusting God to take care of him, man took on the burden of caring for himself. Man's every waking moment was filled with thoughts of "How will I take care of myself?" Man's mind became burdened with care. As described in Matthew 6:25-31, man began to worry about "What will I eat? What will I drink? What will I wear?" His thought life became dominated by worry.

The stress of prolonged worry will result in mental and physical illness; and, it hinders the manifestation of divine health and wholeness. A stressful, worried mind will eventually affect your physical well-being. Dis-ease of the soul will cause disease in the body.

As I stated in the chapter, "Stress", fear is the foundation for stress, and perfect love is the cure for stress. Therefore, **perfect love** is the cure for the stress of worry! As born-again believers, our spirit has been recreated and we now have the attributes of our Father God. Attributes of our new birth includes the perfect love of God and the peace of God. As we built our relationship with God and grow in revelation of His perfect love for us, our trust in God will grow. As our trust in God grows, our peace increases, and worry diminishes. As born-again believers, we are equipped to live the worry-free life that God intended from the beginning.

The body that God created for mankind was not created to take on worry. The only way to stop worrying is to learn to trust God. We learn to trust Him by first seeking the things of

God over seeking anything else. We, as born-again believers, have the privilege to reconnect with God and become totally dependent on Him as our provider, protector, and way-maker. So, while people of the world are filled with worry, we are growing in our trust in God to the point that we will not have a care in this world.

According to Philippians 4:7, born-again believers have the peace of God in them which is far more wonderful than the human mind can understand. In situations where others are worried, we have a peace coming from our born-again spirit that just doesn't make common sense. This type of peace is God's antidote for worry. When we really trust God and take Him at His Word, we stir up the peace that is in our born-again spirit. Total trust in God removes any anxiety about anything that may concern us. As we think on God's love for us, our minds will be at peace.

God lets us know in Isaiah 26:3 that He will keep those in perfect peace whose minds are stayed on Him, because they trust in Him. A peaceful mind results in a peaceful body. As our mind is at peace, every fiber of our being replicates the peace that is in our born-again spirit. We become totally relaxed and at rest because we are trusting in our Father God to confirm His Word concerning whatever situation we are dealing with. Trusting God results in peace; and, the wholeness of our body depends on peace.

We are instructed in Philippians 4:6 to not worry about anything. According to Matthew 6:27, Common English Bible (CEB) version, worrying will not add a single moment to your life. In fact, worry will shorten your life and diminish your quality of life.

Most of us have experienced the stress of worry. We all have faced life challenges which were designed to try to get us to walk in worry. In times like these, we, as born-again believers, can't afford to stress out like people who don't know God. This is what we must do:

- **Focus on God's perfect love.** Focusing on God's love for you builds trust in God. Trusting God eliminates worry.

- **Seek God first.** Matthew 6:33 tells us to make seeking the things of God a higher priority than seeking the solution to the problems you are worried about. As you get caught up in seeking the things of God through His Word rather than worrying, you will notice that every problem that you were worried about is solved.

- **Stir up the peace of God** that is in your born-again spirit by meditating on God's Word. Meditate on scriptures such as, Philippians 4:6,7, John 14:27, and 1 Peter 5:7.

- **Instead of worrying, pray.** Philippians 4:6, 7 Living Bible (TLB) states, *"Don't worry about anything; instead, pray about everything; tell God your needs, and don't forget to thank him for his answers. If you do this, you will experience God's peace, which is far more wonderful than the human mind can understand.*

His peace will keep your thoughts and your hearts quiet and at rest as you trust in Christ Jesus."

- **Lean not to your own understanding.** Invite God into the situation. Don't think that you must figure out everything on your own. People are stressed by worry because they are trying to fix their own problems without consulting God. It is prideful to think you can figure out solutions without God. Pray in the spirit. When you pray in the spirit, you are praying from the wisdom of God; and, you are tapping into the answer to the problem that may be beyond your understanding. There is no need to tackle problems on your own when God is willing and able to help. Proverbs 3:5-6 says, *Trust in the Lord with all thine heart; and lean not unto thine own understanding. ⁶ In all thy ways acknowledge him, and he shall direct thy paths.*

- **Cast all your care on Jesus.** Casting your care is like tossing a ball to another person. When you toss the ball to another person, you no longer have the ball. When you toss your care onto Jesus, you no longer have the care. Listen to the invitation in 1 Peter 5:7 (KJV): *Casting all your care upon him; for he careth for you.* God loves and cares for you. So, get caught up in God's love and become carefree!

- **Trust God completely.** When you trust God completely, there is no room for worry. It is impossible to truly trust God and worry at the same time. When you are trusting

God, you are not worrying. And when you are worrying, you are not trusting God.

- **Praise and worship God.** When you have truly cast your care and you are trusting in God, you will praise God for the solution that He has already accomplished on your behalf. Praise and worship will bring peace to your mind and rest to your body.

- **Be still and know that God is God** (Psalm 46:10). Get quiet before God and listen to His still, small voice within you. He will give you the assurance that everything will be alright.

Worrying–not trusting God–is a BIG deal. It is something that we should not take lightly because worrying is a sin. It is a major reason that God's will is not manifested in our lives. Worry is meditating on the lies of the devil to the point that you believe the devil's words over God's Words. This is what Adam and Eve did, and it caused the fall of mankind. When you worry, you have been deceived. **To have a worry-free life, you must trust God completely.** You must be fully persuaded that God's Word is true. Not trusting God is saying to God, "I don't believe Your Word." Not believing God's Word is actually calling God a liar. Most of us would never, ever let those words come out of our mouth. But our actions may be speaking those words loudly and clearly. When we put more trust in the words of others than in the Word of God, it dishonors Him. When we elevate our feelings or our rational reasoning and perception of things over the Word of God, it is a dishonor to God. Honor

God by trusting Him completely, and you will live a worry-free life which promotes a life of divine health and wholeness.

PRAYER:

Lord, now that I see worry for what it really is – lack of trust in You and Your Word. Forgive me. Lord, show me, me. Don't let me be deceived by not realizing that I am dishonoring You with my thoughts, words or actions that demonstrate a distrust in You. Thank You for forgiving me and alerting me to the deceptive trap of worry. Thank You for giving me Your peace which is far more wonderful than the human mind can understand. Thank You for loving me with Your perfect love. So, I have no need to worry because I can trust You to meet every need in my life. I pray this is Jesus' Name. Amen!

CONFESSION:

I worry for nothing. I trust in God's Word beyond words from any other source. I trust in God's Word beyond my own understanding, perceptions, reasonings, or feelings. I live a worry-free life. I am experiencing a rest and peace that is far more wonderful than the human mind can understand because I trust God completely. I don't have a care in the world. Therefore, I live a life of divine health and wholeness.

PERSONAL THOUGHTS:

_____

_____

_____

_____

_____

_____

_____

_____

_____

_____

_____

_____

_____

_____

_____

_____

_____

DAY 18

Unforgiveness

Scriptures:

Ephesians 4:32 The Message (MSG) ... *Be gentle with one another, sensitive. Forgive one another as quickly and thoroughly as God in Christ forgave you.*

Matthew 5:44 (KJV)–I say unto you, Love your enemies, bless them that curse you, do good to them that hate you, and pray for them which despitefully use you, and persecute you;

Romans 12:20 (KJV) Therefore if thine enemy hunger, feed him; if he thirst, give him drink: for in so doing thou shalt heap coals of fire on his head.

Luke 23:34 (NIV)–Jesus said, "Father, forgive them, for they do not know what they are doing."

Are there people you know, when you encounter them, they take the smile right off your face, cause your eyes to roll, your nostrils to flare, and your heart to change its beat? Sarcastically, you may say, "He/She makes me sick!" This statement may be more than just sarcasm; it may be a fact. When you are holding resentment or unforgiveness towards a person, that person can *literally* make you sick. Unforgiveness is a detriment to your walking in health and wholeness.

As a result of man's broken relationship with God, man's relationship with people became broken. Broken relationships with people cause stress to manifest as **unforgiveness**. Man developed an unforgiving heart towards his fellow man, which resulted in resentment, jealousy, strife, bitterness, hatred, and murder. Unforgiveness stirs up envy and strife. According to James 3:16, where envying and strife is, there is confusion and every evil work. Unforgiveness causes people to hold on to offenses and harbor hurts of the past. Unforgiveness can open the door for the enemy to work destruction in your life and hinder the abundant life that Jesus came for you to have.

As with the stress of worry, the cure for the stress of unforgiveness is **perfect love**. Therefore, to be free of unforgiveness, one must practice walking in perfect love which is the God kind of love. To walk in perfect love, you must realize these three truths:

1. God loves you with His perfect love.
2. As a child of God, you have God's perfect love in you.
3. With God's perfect love in you, you have the capacity to love and forgive others as God loves and forgives you.

As born-again believers, **God's love in us** equips us to love and forgive others. We can forgive others just as God has forgiven us. As we build our relationship with God, the attribute of love that we inherited from Him will be manifested in our relationships with others, causing unforgiveness to be broken off our lives. We are equipped to live a lifestyle of forgiveness.

Most of us have experienced the stress of unforgiveness. We all have faced offenses which were designed to get us to walk in unforgiveness. I believe we are most like Jesus when we forgive those who have offended us. None of us have been offended to the degree that Jesus was offended. In Luke 23:34, we find Jesus' response to the greatest of all offenses,

Jesus said, "Father, forgive them, for they do not know what they are doing."

One may say, "Well, that was Jesus, the Son of God. Maybe He could forgive like that, but I can't." Yes, you can! If you are born-again, you are a child of God. Just like Jesus, you have that perfect love within you to enable you to forgive any offense. We have choices. Since we have the power within us to forgive, it is just a matter of choice. We can choose to forgive, or we can choose not to forgive. Once we make the decision to forgive, the perfect love that is in our born-again spirit will rise up big, enabling us to do what is humanly impossible. Unforgiveness will be annihilated and perfect love will take over.

If you want to walk in health and wholeness, you can't afford to live a lifestyle of unforgiveness. This is what you must do:

- **Focus on the perfect love of God within you** that equips you to love and forgive others. Meditate on scriptures that will stir up the love of God that is in you.
- **Pray for the person who hurt or offended you.** According to Matthew 5:44, *pray for them which despitefully use you and persecute you.* In addition to praying in your understanding, pray in the spirit. When you pray in the spirit, you are praying from the wisdom of God and you are tapping into the real needs of that person who hurt you. There is no need to tackle offenses on your own when God is willing and able to help. When you pray, you are tapping into the perfect love of God inside you.
- **Forgive offenses quickly.** Ephesians 4:32 The Message (MSG) states – *"Be gentle with one another, sensitive. Forgive one another as quickly and thoroughly as God in Christ forgave you."* Remember, you have ability within your born-again spirit to walk in the love of God and to forgive others, just as God has forgiven you.
- **Perform an act of kindness for the person who has offended you.** According to Romans 12:20, *if the offender is hungry, feed him, if he thirst, give him a drink.* I know in the natural this is hard to do; but, keep in mind, you can operate in the supernatural since you have God's divine nature in you which enables you to do what is naturally impossible.

- **Praise and worship God** for taking care of the broken relationship. Praise God for the solution He has already accomplished on your behalf.

PRAYER:

Help me Lord, to see myself. Show me any area of my life where I have allowed unforgiveness to enter. Lord, forgive me for the sin of unforgiveness. I know when I don't forgive, I am opening my life up to envy, strife, confusion, and every evil work. So, I choose to forgive by Your perfect love which is in me. I now pray in the spirit over the situations that tempt me to walk in unforgiveness. When I pray in the spirit, I am allowing the Holy Spirit to speak Your perfect will through me for these situations. Thank You, Lord, for loving me with Your perfect love and enabling me, with Your perfect love within my born-again spirit, to remove unforgiveness from my life. I pray this in Jesus' Name. Amen!

CONFESSION:

I realize unforgiveness is sin. I make the quality decision to resist temptations to walk in unforgiveness. God loves me and has equipped me with the ability to love and forgive others. So, I am quick to forgive. I am following Jesus' example, and I am living a life of love and forgiveness which promotes the divine health and wholeness that my Father God intends for me.

PERSONAL THOUGHTS:

_____

_____

_____

_____

_____

_____

_____

_____

_____

_____

_____

_____

_____

_____

_____

_____

_____

DAY 19

Embracing Sickness

Scripture:

James 1:6-7 New Living Translation (NLT)

⁶ But when you ask him, be sure that your faith is in God alone. Do not waver, for a person with divided loyalty is as unsettled as a wave of the sea that is blown and tossed by the wind. ⁷ Such people should not expect to receive anything from the Lord.

I am convinced that there are situations where sicknesses stay with people because they use them for selfish benefits. Sometimes, people pray for healing, but they also embrace the benefits that sickness can bring. They are torn between the desire to get well immediately or to get all the perks they can out of being sick. There are two major selfish benefits of being sick. The first is the benefit of getting attention from others. The second is the benefit of having an excuse to get out of doing something that they don't want to do.

Many times, using sickness to get attention from others is a behavior learned in childhood. Oftentimes, children get great attention from their parents when they are sick. Most mothers will pamper a sick child. Separated parents will come together to rally around a sick child. Therefore, at a young age, many children learn that there are great benefits in being sick. Even as adults, people use sickness to get attention. A spouse may use it to get attention from the other spouse. Some church members use sickness to get attention from their pastor and other church members. When people are sick, others visit, bring food, and clean their house. Children and grandchildren spend time with them. For many, this self-centered attention is better than being well. Sickness becomes a tool to manipulate others into doing what we want them to do.

The second selfish benefit of being sick is having an excuse to get out of doing something that you don't want to do. Sickness is always the acceptable excuse. Again, as a child, we learn that if we don't want to do something, sickness will get us out of doing it. Many children learn that if they are sick, they don't have to go to school or do chores. They carry this same behavior into adulthood. Instead of resisting and attacking a symptom with the Word of God and prayer, some see it as a perfect excuse to get out of doing something they don't want to do. People will use a symptom of sickness to get out of going to work. They think, "Well, I won't resist this sickness today because I can use it to get a day off." Our *immediate* response to sickness should always be to resist it and attack it with the Word of God and prayer.

I recall a situation where a Christian man cleaning the building where I worked told me about a foot surgery that he was going to get due to complication from diabetes. I told him that I would be in prayer for him. He immediately responded, "Don't pray too hard because I expect to be able to go on disability because of this." This man embraced sickness as a means to get early retirement.

I recall another situation where a dear Christian lady felt that God was leading her to leave the church where she had attended her whole life. To please the people of the church, she stopped going to church, using sickness as the excuse for not attending church. She had been standing in faith for her healing, but now sickness became a way to leave the church and at the same time save face with the people of the church. Needless to say, this lady did not see the manifestation of her healing.

These selfish benefits cause people to embrace sickness rather than resist it. They pray and allow others to pray for them, but their prayers are hindered by the half-hearted commitment to receiving their healing. According to James 1:6-7, people who pray in this manner will not receive anything from the Lord. They are divided between wanting to be healed and wanting to enjoy the benefits of being sick. If you find yourself embracing sickness for any reason, remember that it is God's will for you to walk in health and wholeness; and, the will of God is more beneficial than any selfish benefit we may receive from being sick.

PRAYER:

Lord, forgive me if I have embraced sickness for any reason. I know that sickness is not from You, and I refuse to embrace anything that is not from You. Lord, forgive me for manipulating people or situations for my own selfish benefits. I thank You for correcting my wrong way of thinking. I receive Your forgiveness. Thank You, Lord, for loving me and for providing health and wholeness for me. I pray this in Jesus' Name. Amen!

CONFESSION:

I refuse to embrace sickness for selfish benefits. I refuse to use sickness as means to manipulate people or situations. If I am attacked with a symptom of sickness, I will IMMEDIATELY attack it with the Word of God and prayer. I will receive the health and wholeness that God has provided.

PERSONAL THOUGHTS:

_____

_____

_____

_____

_____

_____

_____

_____

_____

_____

_____

_____

_____

_____

_____

_____

_____

_____

_____

DAY 20

Blaming God

Scripture:

> **John 10:10**–*The thief cometh not, but for to steal, and to kill, and to destroy: I am come that they might have life, and that they might have it more abundantly.*

The devil is characterized as the thief in John 10:10. There is a real devil. I am amazed that some Christians totally ignore the works of the devil. I believe that one of the greatest weapons of the devil is that he works undetected and totally ignored as being at the core of a problem. There were times in Jesus' earthly ministry where he would cast out the devil before healing the sick. Many times, God gets the blame for what the devil is doing. Sickness has been attributed to God trying to teach someone something or God punishing someone, while totally ignoring that the devil is the one who steals, kills, and destroys. Anything that is stealing your health and killing and destroying your body according to John 10:10 the devil is the source. Jesus came that we might have life and not just life, but an abundant life. An abundant life is a healthy, vibrant, thriving life – a divinely healthy and whole life.

One reason many people don't fight against sickness is because they are convinced that it is God's will for them to be sick, and God has a good reason for putting the sickness on them. If you are sick, know that God did not put that sickness on you. God is not the source of sickness. It is God's will for you to be well. He loves you and sickness is not a part of His plan for your life. So, don't settle for sickness. Don't allow it to continue to dominate your life. Resist it! Jesus came to give us abundant life. Receive what Jesus came to give.

The idea that God would put sickness on people to teach a lesson is giving sickness the role of the Holy Spirit. According to John 14:26, the Holy Spirit is the teacher. During a sickness we can learn some beneficial lessons **if we trust God**. In challenging situations, God can take what the devil meant for our destruction and turn it to our good. When we don't trust God in challenging situations, the situation can lead to devastation and total destruction. So, if there is a lesson learned during an illness, it is by revelation of the Word of God, the leading of the Holy Spirit, and the goodness of God. Therefore, give God, not sickness, the glory for any lesson that you may learn during a time of illness.

Some may say, "Okay, I agree. God did not put sickness on me, but He allowed it." When we say that, we are still trying to shift the blame to God. The truth of the matter is that **we** allowed it. Look at Matthew 16:19 in the Contemporary English Version (CEV).

I will give you the keys to the kingdom of heaven, and God in heaven will allow whatever you allow on earth. But he will not allow anything that you don't allow.

The question is, what are we allowing? What are we putting up with and tolerating in our lives?

God has done everything necessary for us to live whole, healthy lives. He sent his only begotten Son Jesus to take the stripes on his physical body for the healing of our physical bodies. He sent His Word to heal us. He sent His Holy Spirit to lead and guide us in truths concerning walking in divine health. And He gave us authority over all the works of the devil according to Luke 10:19.

So, don't blame God for sickness. Instead, give God the glory for making provision for your divine health and wholeness.

PRAYER:

Father God, thank You so much for sending Jesus to provide abundant life for me. An abundant life is a healthy, vibrant, thriving life – a divinely-healthy and whole life. Forgive me if I have attributed the works of the devil to You. I now know that anything that is stealing my health or killing and destroying my body is not from You. Thank You for loving me so much that You would provide abundant life for me! I receive the abundant life that You are offering to me.

I pray this in Jesus' Name. Amen.

CONFESSION:

Jesus has provided an abundant life for me. Sickness and disease are not a part of God's plan for my life. I refuse anything that is trying to steal my health or kill and destroy my body. I only receive those things that Jesus has provided for me. I receive an abundant life of divine health and wholeness.

PERSONAL THOUGHTS:

DAY 21

Why Didn't That "Good Person" Get Healed?

Scripture:

Matthew 9:29 (KJV)

... According to your faith be it unto you.

How do most of us define a "good person"? When defining a good person, we look at that person's deeds. A good person is known for doing good deeds and godly acts. They treat people well and show great kindness. They are willing to assist in meeting the needs of others. They demonstrate a godly character by exhibiting the fruit of the Spirit in their lives such as love, patience, kindness, goodness, and gentleness. So, we may think, when a person of such character is attacked with sickness, surely that person deserves to be healed. So, when we pray for the healing a "good person", and healing does not manifest, we may be at a loss to understand what happened. Many begin to doubt God's Word concerning healing. Some even come up with all types of philosophies as to why healing didn't take place. We hear ideas such as, "It was not God's will for that person to be healed.", "God picks and chooses who He will heal", "Healing takes place only in heaven." or, "That person must not have been as good as we thought he/she was."

The truth is, it is not our good deeds, kind acts, or godly character that causes us to be healed. Healing has already been provided for everyone through the finished work of Jesus. All we have to do to receive healing is to believe. Jesus said, "According to your faith be it unto you." No matter how good you are, if you don't believe, you won't receive. Search the scriptures concerning Jesus' healing ministry; never will you find where Jesus went through an inventory of a person's good deeds before healing them. If a person has never done a good deed in his/her life, but hears God's Word concerning healing and truly believes that Word, that person will be healed. We don't receive healing based on how good we are or on what good deeds we have done, but on what we truly believe in our heart. Performing good deeds is a noble thing to do; however, doing good deeds is not what qualifies us to be healed. It is by believing God's Word concerning healing and confessing it with our mouth that causes healing to manifest.

There may be people who have demonstrated the exemplary Christian life and may have been used as instruments in getting others healed; but, when it came to their own healing, they were not able to receive. Many times, after great men and women of God die of sicknesses, those following them and who were standing in faith for their personal healing, will stop believing. Some will say, "That great person of God did not get healed, so why should I think someone like me has the chance to be healed" and will let go of their faith for healing.

It is not about that someone has lived such a good life that they deserve to be healed. Nor is it that a person has lived a bad life that they do not deserve to be healed. Some may think that they are not good enough to be healed; but, James 5:15 tells us, *"The prayer of faith will save the sick, and the Lord will raise him up. And if he has committed sins, he will be forgiven."* Forgiveness has been provided along with healing. Isn't Jesus WONDERFUL! Jesus took sickness on his body for ALL to be healed. **It is not about what we have done; it is all about what Jesus did.** Anyone who truly believes in what Jesus did will be healed.

All born-again believers have "the" measure of faith, according to Romans 12:3. What you develop your faith for is how you will use your faith. Faith is developed by hearing the Word of God. I have seen sick people develop their faith for healing, others develop faith for contentment, and yet others develop their faith for departing this world and going to heaven.

Many develop faith for contentment in situations where they have prayed for healing and it has not manifested. They begin to think that it is God's will for them to be sick; so, they just need to be content and ask for strength to bear the sickness. They seek God to help them with the daily struggle of dealing with the sickness and all hope has gone that they will ever see a manifestation of healing. They begin to believe and say, "Okay, Lord, since healing has not manifested, it must be Your will for me to bear this sickness. Therefore, I am believing You for the strength to bear this sickness." I have seen this prayer answered over and over again. God will meet you where you apply your faith. If you are believing God for strength to endure, He will give you the strength. Many will say, "I don't understand how that person is so peaceful, joyful, and content in spite of their physical condition." This strength is the supernatural answer to their prayer of faith.

Yet there are others who have prayed for healing and have not seen a manifestation, but they are not content with just bearing a sickness that has greatly interfered with their quality of life. Many times, these individuals will apply their faith to departing this world and going to heaven where there is no sickness or disease. They focus on the scriptures concerning death of the saints and on what has been prepared for them in heaven. They get peace and contentment for departing from this world and being present with the Lord in heaven. They aim their desire and prayer on the joys of being in heaven.

Whatever you apply your faith to, that is where you will have the victory. I believe there is a good, acceptable, and perfect will of God. It may be God's good will for one to gain the strength to bear a sickness. It may be His acceptable will for one to escape the sickness by leaving this world and going to heaven. But I believe it is His perfect will for your body to be totally healed and made whole from any attack of sickness or disease with a full manifestation of His supernatural healing power.

It is okay if we choose to use our faith for strength to bear a sickness or to be with our Father God in heaven. God gave us faith to use as we so choose. As Jesus said, "According to **your** faith be it unto you." It's your faith; use it however you please.

Therefore, to look at good people who were not physically healed of their sickness and conclude that God's Word concerning healing doesn't work is a huge mistake. God's Word is the truth, and the truth never changes. Healing is not about your good deeds or how deserving you may be. It is about what you truly believe in your heart and to what you have chosen to apply your faith. It is hard to know the heart of another person. The question is this: What do you believe in your heart, and how are you applying your faith? It is your choice.

PRAYER:

Father God, thank You for showing me that by Your grace, You have provided healing and wholeness for everyone–not based on our deeds, but based on the stripes of Jesus. Thank You for giving me "the" measure of faith and for giving me Your Word so I can develop my faith. Help me to develop my faith to walk in your perfect will concerning health and wholeness.

I pray this in Jesus' Name. Amen!

CONFESSION:

I will keep my eyes on God's Word. I will not allow my perception of the personal experiences of others to make me doubt God's Word. I will develop "the" measure of faith that

God has given me to cause His perfect will concerning health and wholeness to manifest in my life.

PERSONAL THOUGHTS:

Biblical Foundations for Divine Health and Wholeness

Proverbs 4:20-22
The Passion Translation (TPT)

*²⁰ Listen carefully, my dear child, to everything that I
teach you,
and pay attention to all that I have to say.
²¹ Fill your thoughts with my words
until they penetrate deep into your spirit.
²² Then, as you unwrap my words,
they will impart true life and radiant health
into the very core of your being.*

Matthew 7:24
The Passion Translation (TPT)
*Everyone who hears my teaching and applies it to his life
can be compared to a wise man who built his house on an
unshakable foundation.*

DAY 22

Truth, Facts and Lies

Scriptures:

> *John 17:17 (KJV)–Sanctify them through thy truth: **thy word is truth**.*

> *1 Thessalonians 2:13(KJV)–For this cause also thank we God without ceasing, because, when ye received the word of God which ye heard of us, ye received it not as the word of men, but **as it is in truth, the word of God**, which effectually worketh also in you that believe.*

> *2 Corinthians 4;18 (KJV) While we look not at the things which are seen, but at the things which are not seen: for the things which are seen are temporal; but the things which are not seen are eternal.*

> *John 8:44 (KJV)–Ye are of your father the devil, and the lusts of your father ye will do. He was a*

murderer from the beginning, and abode not in the truth, because there is no truth in him. When he speaketh a lie, he speaketh of his own: for he is a liar, and the father of it.

Numbers 23:19 New Life Version (NLV)–*God is not a man, that He should lie. He is not a son of man, that He should be sorry for what He has said. Has He said, and will He not do it? Has He spoken, and will He not keep His Word?*

John 8:32 Modern English Version (MEV)– *You shall know the truth, and the truth shall set you free.*

Truth, facts, and lies are words that we deal with daily. The way we define these words can have a profound effect on the way we live our lives and on whether or not we walk in divine health and wholeness. The way we deal with people, situations, and problems all have to do with what we perceive as being truth, facts, and lies. How we classify something as being a truth, fact or lie, is the basis for our decision-making process. Our decisions dictate the way we live our lives.

In many arenas it is believed that facts indicate the truth. In a court of law, cases are judged on the premise that facts lead to the truth. If facts indicate a certain conclusion, then that conclusion is assumed to be true. The same logic is applied in medical science. Medical science is based on facts. Conclusions are drawn from facts that are gathered by observing what is physically detectable through experimentation and examination. Doctors make diagnoses based on comparing these facts with previous observations. Treatment is based on the assumption that the diagnosis is the truth.

Just as in a court of law and in medical science, many of us make judgment calls every day based on collecting facts through our observations. Based on these facts, along with rational reasoning, we conclude what we believe to be the truth or a lie. Many of our everyday decisions are made on the premise of collecting facts to find the truth.

Since we make life decisions based on the way we define truth, facts, and lies, it is imperative that we have a correct definition of these terms. Here we are going to give the definition of these terms, not from a dictionary, but from the Word of God. By applying to your life how the Word of God defines these terms, your life will be revolutionized. When it comes to your walking in divine health and wholeness, it is vitally important that you have a clear understanding of what is meant by truth, lies and facts.

What is truth?

Truth is Holy Spirit-inspired Word of God. It is impossible to define truth apart from the Word of God. According to John 17:17, **God's Word is truth (God's Word = Truth)**. In many passages in the Bible (II Timothy 2:15, James 1:18, Ephesians 1:13, II Corinthians 6:7, Psalm 119:43), God's Word is referred

143

to as the **Word of Truth**. God's Word is absolute and never-changing. Therefore, truth is absolute and never-changing.

What is a lie?

A **lie** is anything contrary to the Word of God. Lies are thoughts, words, ideas, concepts, or circumstances that contradict the Word of God. According to John 8:44, lies are equivalent to the words of the devil, just as truth is equivalent to the Word of God. The devil cannot speak the truth (John 8:44), just as God cannot lie (Numbers 23:14).

What is a fact?

A **fact** is physical evidence detected by the five senses. Facts are things we can see, hear, smell, taste, and feel. Facts are based on human observation and perception of the world. Facts can be used to draw conclusions. According to 2 Corinthians 4:18, things that are seen (detectable by the five senses) are temporal; that is, facts are subject to change. Facts can support the truth or support a lie. When facts bring you to a conclusion that contradicts the Word of God, then the facts support a lie. When facts bring you to a conclusion that lines up with the Word of God, then the facts support the truth.

Let's look at two examples from the Word of God identifying truth, facts and lies.

In Genesis chapters 37 through 45 is an example that clearly identifies truth, facts, and lies. God promised Joseph that his brothers would bow down to him. His brothers sold him into slavery and presented his bloody coat to their father as fact that Joseph had been killed by a wild animal. Joseph's father took the fact of the bloody coat and concluded that Joseph had been killed to be the truth. Here the fact supported a lie and not the truth. Since God's Word is the truth, Joseph could not have died because God promised that Joseph's brothers would bow down to him. As you follow the story, Joseph became a ruler in Egypt and his brothers did bow down to him. Here we can see that facts were changed to line up with the truth, but the truth never changed.

Romans Chapter 4 describes another example identifying truth, facts, and lies. Romans 4:19, 20, 21 reads as follows:

> *And being not weak in faith, [Abraham] considered not his own body now dead, when he was about an hundred years old, neither yet the deadness of Sarah's womb; He staggered not at the promise of God through unbelief; but was strong in faith, giving glory to God; And being fully persuaded that, what he had promised, he was able also to perform.*

Abraham ignored contradicting facts and embraced the truth. The truth was the promise from God that he and Sarah would produce a child. The facts were that Abraham and Sarah were old in age and their bodies did not have the physical functionality for a child to be conceived. In this case, facts supported a lie because the facts supported an outcome that was contrary to the Word of God. Abraham did not consider the symptoms that manifested in his and Sarah's physical bodies. He was not distracted by facts that did not agree with the truth; instead, he was fully persuaded by the truth of God's Word. Therefore, the facts had to change and line up with the truth. Abraham and Sarah did produce the child that God promised. Abraham is called the "father of faith" because he walked by faith in the truth and not by contradicting facts.

Now, based on the Word of God, here are some nuggets we can conclude about truth, facts, and lies.

- According to II Corinthians 5:7, *"For we walk by faith and not by sight."* Walking by faith is building our lives around the truth of God's Word. Walking by sight is building our lives around facts. Facts are temporal and subject to change. Truth is eternal and will never change. When you build your life on the truth, you have a solid foundation. Building your life on facts is like building on shifting sand.
- In faith, we don't deny facts; but, we hold truth to be a higher authority than facts. Facts are subject to change. In faith, we embrace the truth which never changes. When we are fully persuaded by the truth of God's Word, facts that appear to contradict the truth will have

to change and come into agreement with the truth. You see, truth changes facts. But it is impossible for facts to change truth.

- According to John 8:32 (MEV), *"You shall know the truth, and the truth shall set you free."* It is the truth that you believe to the point that you know it and have no doubts about it, that will set you free. The truth of God's Word will set you free from the bondage of being limited to what you can see–that is, being limited to facts. When facts are not lining up with the Word of God, the truth that you know will cause you to surpass natural barriers and tap into the supernatural power of God.

- Romans 4:17 states that God calls those things that be not as though they were. In the natural, it sounds as if God is lying. But we must look at this from God's perspective. This is how God created the world, calling into existence things that did not exist in the physical realm. We should always believe and speak the truth, even when there is no factual support for it. By doing this, we are calling truth into factual existence. We just can't conclude that what we see manifested is all there is. When we believe the Word of truth in our heart and speak it with our mouth, contradicting facts will eventually support the truth.

- Put highest value on truth. Embrace the truth, cherish the truth, and love the truth. Whenever you find the truth of God's Word, hold fast to it, don't let it go. Stand on it. Believe it. Find the truth concerning every situation in your life and put it in your heart. Let it become dear to you. Treasure it. And don't let anyone or anything take it away from you.

Now, let's apply what we have learned about truth, facts, and lies to walking in divine health and wholeness.

God has given to us five senses to be able to detect the physical world around us and gather facts which are helpful and necessary to maintain life in this physical world. As stated earlier, medical science is based in facts. So, we can see that facts can be beneficial. But God did not limit us to just using physically detectable facts to figure out how to survive in this physical world. God has also given to us the truth. If we only consider facts, we will never walk in the divine superabundant health and wholeness that God intends for us to walk in.

Facts, may say, "Your head hurts. Your eyesight is blurred. Your Dad died of cancer. Your relatives have short life spans. Your ethnic group is subject to diabetes. Your blood pressure is high. You have heart failure. Your kidneys are not functioning properly. You have stage-4 cancer." All of these are facts which are physical evidence that can be detected by human observation.

Facts can be used as a predictor of the future. Based on facts, you may make predictions about your future, such as, "I will never lose this weight. This headache is never going away. I will have to learn to live with this pain. I am going the die of the same disease as my mother." Based on facts, a medical professional may draw conclusions about your future, such as,

"Your disease is incurable. You will be on medication for the rest of your life. You have six months to live."

STOP! Before you get caught up in all these predictions, find out what the Word of God has to say about your health and wholeness. Keep in mind, God's Word is the truth.

Truth says —

- God sent His Word and healed you (Psalm 107:20).
- God heals all diseases (Psalm 103:3).
- God redeems your life from destruction (Psalm 103:4).
- God renews your youth (Psalm 103:5).
- God satisfies you with a long life (Psalm 91:16).
- God will take sickness away from your midst (Exodus 23:25).
- God's will is for you to be in health (3 John 2).
- The same power that raised Jesus' body from the dead is in your body, quickening your mortal body (Romans 8:11).
- Jesus has redeemed you from the curse of sickness and disease (Galatians 3:13).
- By the stripes Jesus took on His body, your body is healed (Isaiah 53:5, I Peter 2:24).
- Jesus came that you might have an abundant life (John 10:10).

This is the truth about you. Anything contrary is a lie!

You must speak the truth over your life in order to have a long healthy life. Recall the definition of a lie – anything contrary to the Word of God. Be careful not to speak lies over your life, that is, do not speak anything concerning your life that is contrary to the Word of God. Medical professionals may speak facts that are contrary to the Word of God. But what are YOU saying? It is your words that you speak and believe over your life that is manifested in your life. Make sure you are speaking the truth over your life, and not lies. Look at 1 Peter 3:10 (VOICE):

> *If you love life and want to live a good, long life*
> *Then be careful what you say. Don't tell lies...*

As you embrace the truth and resist lies concerning your health and wholeness, contradicting facts will have to change and line up with the truth. The truth of the matter is, "It is God's will for you to walk in divine superabundant health and wholeness all the days of your life!"

PRAYER:

Father God, thank You so much for the truth. Your Word is truth. And the truth sets me free. I am free from the bondage of limiting my life to just facts. Thank You for the health and wholeness that Your Word of Truth has promised through the stripes of Jesus. When it appears that facts concerning my health are not lining up with the truth, help me to embrace truth. Help me to always esteem truth higher than contradicting facts and resist the lies of the enemy. Thank You that Your Word of Truth has provided for me divine superabundant health and wholeness.

I pray this in Jesus' Name. Amen!

CONFESSION:

I will always agree with the what the Truth says about me even in the face of contradicting facts and lies of the enemy.

Truth says —-

- God sent His Word and healed me (Psalm 107:20).
- God heals all diseases (Psalm 103:3).
- God redeems my life from destruction (Psalm 103:4).
- God renews my youth (Psalm 103:5).
- God satisfies me with a long life (Psalm 91:16).
- God will take sickness away from my midst (Exodus 23:25).
- God's will is for me to be in health (3 John 2).
- The same power that raised Jesus' body from the dead is in your body, quickening my mortal body (Romans 8:11).
- Jesus has redeemed me from the curse of sickness and disease (Galatians 3:13).
- By the stripes Jesus took on His body, my body is healed (Isaiah 53:5, I Peter 2:24).
- Jesus came that I might have an abundant life (John 10:10),

This is the truth about me. Anything contrary is a lie. As I embrace the truth and resist lies concerning my health and wholeness, contradicting facts will have to change and line up with the truth. The truth of the matter is, "It is God's will for me to walk in divine superabundant health and wholeness all the days of my life!"

PERSONAL THOUGHTS:

_____

_____

_____

_____

_____

_____

_____

_____

_____

_____

_____

_____

_____

_____

_____

_____

_____

_____

DAY 23

It Pleases God for Me to Receive

Scripture:

Hebrews 11:6 (KJV)

> *⁶ But without faith it is impossible to please him: for he that cometh to God must believe that he is, and that he is a rewarder of them that diligently seek him.*

Many see getting healed as struggling with God–as though we've got to wrestle healing out of God's hand. But your struggle is not with God. Your struggle is with fear, doubt, and unbelief. God is on your side! God is on the side of healing. He wants you healed more than you want to be healed. Healing is God's idea. He demonstrated this by allowing His Son Jesus to take on His body the stripes for our healing. Healing is God's desire for you; and even more than it being His desire for you, it pleases Him for you to receive healing. If you really want to please God, trust Him enough to receive everything He has provided for you and is offering to you. Hebrews 11:6 states,

"But without faith it is impossible to please him..." Faith is trusting God by believing His Word, knowing that He is not a man that would lie.

I remember watching a Christian television program where a lady was testifying concerning her divine healing from colon cancer. This is what struck me to my heart concerning her testimony: She said that she was thanking God for healing her when God interrupted and said, "Thank you for receiving." Just think, God was thanking her for receiving her healing. Like a light bulb switching on, it dawned on me that it pleases God for us to receive from Him. At that moment I could almost feel the frustration and distress that God must feel when we don't receive from Him. God loves us so much, and He has made provision for us to live an abundant life of divine health. He has provided healing through the stripes of Jesus. I can just see God overjoyed with contentment, singing, dancing, and laughing when a person receives the healing and wholeness that He so desires for him/her to have. I can see His joy being so contagious that all of heaven rejoices; the angels and the great cloud of witnesses who have preceded us to heaven are rejoicing. I can see our loved ones in heaven saying, "Praise God, they received!"

It pleases God for us to trust Him wholeheartedly. Remember, without faith it is impossible to please God; and, without faith you cannot receive from God. In fact, it disrespects God when you don't receive from Him because you are showing a lack of trust in Him. I recall an incident with my grandmother where I demonstrated a lack of trust in her. When I was around three years of age, my mother went into the hospital, and I stayed with my paternal grandmother. During the time I was with her, she would prepare meals and set a plate before me at the kitchen table; but, I refused to eat. To say the least, my grandmother became quite frustrated with my behavior. What she did not know is that my mother was very particular about cleanliness. When we would visit people, some people had houses that met my mother's standard of cleanliness, and others did not. As a part of southern hospitality, people would always offer visitors something to eat. So, my mother made the blanket rule – "Don't trust anybody's cleanliness. So, if you are offered food, just say, no thanks." But what my mother forgot to tell me before going into the hospital is that for this long visit with my grandmother, I had permission to eat. So, since I didn't trust the cleanliness of my grandmother, I refused to eat. She was very displeased with me; and, I am sure she would have been even more displeased with me if she knew that the reason that I was not eating was a lack of faith in her cleanliness. So, just think how displeasing it must be for God when he sets a plate of healing before us, and we refuse it. Keep in mind, unlike my grandmother, God is fully aware that our lack of receiving is a result of our lack of faith in Him.

If you really want to please God, receive your healing! Put away fear, doubt, and unbelief; and, just trust God with your whole heart. Become fully persuaded that God's Word is true. God has already provided healing through the finished works of Jesus. By Jesus' stripes you are healed. Now, God is offering healing to you. So, give God great pleasure by receiving!

PRAYER:

Lord, I thank You so much for providing and offering divine health to me. Lord, I repent of any fear, doubt, or unbelief in my heart that keeps me from receiving from You. Help me to receive. Show me anything that is in my heart that may cause me not to receive. Thank you for showing me that it pleases You for me to receive from You. Thank You for loving me so much that You would take great pleasure in my being healed and whole. I pray this in Jesus' Name. Amen.

CONFESSION:

I receive the divine supernatural health that God is offering to me. I receive the healing provided by the stripes of Jesus. I receive from You, Father God, because it pleases You for me to receive.

PERSONAL THOUGHTS:

_____

_____

_____

_____

_____

_____

_____

_____

_____

_____

_____

_____

_____

_____

_____

_____

_____

_____

_____

DAY 24

Satisfy My Mouth with Good Things

Scriptures:

Psalms 103:2 and 5

2 Bless the LORD, O my soul, and forget not all his benefits:

5 Who satisfieth thy mouth with good things; so that thy youth is renewed like the eagle's.

One of the benefits of belonging to God is that He will satisfy your mouth with good things so that your youth will be renewed. What an awesome benefit! God will make you satisfied eating those things that are good for you so that you will have a healthy, strong, youthful body no matter what your age may be.

Have you ever noticed that most of the time, the body craves things that are not good for it? Most children, if given a choice between candy and spinach, would choose candy. The body has a way of not being satisfied with foods that will do it good. Many of us are not satisfied with the spinach, broccoli, or carrots; and, we will not be satisfied until we get that piece of chocolate cake, ice cream, soda, potato chips, cookies, or fried chicken. However, Psalms 103 informs us that God can change our cravings and make us satisfied eating things that are good for us.

Use this scripture to stand against cravings for things that will harm your body. So many people say while eating, "I know I shouldn't be eating this." Even though they know that something is bad for them, they eat it anyway. I have heard the saying, "If you know better, you will do better." In many cases, this is not true. Many people know that certain foods or drinks are not good for them, but they are not satisfied until they get them. So, the next time you have the desire to drive thirty minutes across town to get that cheese cake that you know you don't need, remember the benefit that God will make you satisfied eating and drinking those things that are good for you so that your youth will be restored. Stand on this benefit to bring the cravings of your body under control. Speak it out loud to your body. Say, "No, body! You line up with the Word of God. You will be totally satisfied eating and drinking those things that are good for you, in Jesus' Name." The scripture, Psalm 103:5, is great to use if you are having problems with food or alcohol addictions.

PRAYER:

[*Identify those things that you crave to eat or drink that you know are not good for you.*]

Father God, I ask You to change my cravings for those things that are not good for my body *[name those things that you just identified].* Make me satisfied eating and drinking those things that are good for me. I ask for Your help because I cannot do this on my own. I thank you, Lord, for Your benefit of making me satisfied eating those things that are good for me so that I may be strong, youthful, and whole. I pray this in Jesus' Name. Amen!

CONFESSION:

[*Speak to your body*] Body, you will be totally satisfied eating and drinking those things that are good for you, in Jesus' Name.

I am satisfied eating those things that are good for me. I do not crave those things that will harm my body. Therefore, my body is strong and healthy, and my youth is renewed.

PERSONAL THOUGHTS:

_____

_____

_____

_____

_____

_____

_____

_____

_____

_____

_____

_____

_____

_____

_____

_____

_____

_____

_____

DAY 25

If You Ingest Any Deadly Thing

Scripture:

Mark 16:17-18 King James Version (KJV)

¹⁷ And these signs shall follow them that believe ...

¹⁸ ... if they drink any deadly thing, it shall not hurt them ...

Many are concerned about the quality of our food and water. The use of pesticides and genetic modification, or simply the quality of our water and air, can make what we ingest in our bodies cause us harm. Even if we make great efforts to eat healthy, there may be chemicals creeping into our food and water supply which can be deadly to our bodies. Another way we may ingest deadly things is through medication. Many times, medication used to fix one problem can cause other deadly problems in the body. Well, God has taken care of these problems. The Word of God has an antidote for any problem we face. Mark 16:18 declares that one of the signs that follow us as believers in Jesus Christ is that if we unknowingly ingest any deadly thing into our bodies, it will not hurt us. Praise God!

God so wants us to live in divine health that He did not leave one stone overturned. He is always looking out for our well-being and provides protection for us from hidden dangers. God will bless our food and water and take sickness away from our midst according to Exodus 23:25. God will go to great lengths to take sickness away from our midst, even to the point of supernaturally causing our bodies not to have normal natural reactions to deadly ingredients. Isn't God amazing!

As you sit down to eat a meal or to take medication, remember to declare God's promise that if you ingest any deadly thing, it will not hurt you. God wants you well and whole!

PRAYER:

Father God, I praise You that You are always looking out for my well-being and for providing protection for me from hidden dangers. Thank You for protecting me from deadly substances that may be in my food, water, or medications. I praise You that You will not allow anything deadly that I may ingest to harm me. Thank You! Thank You! Thank You!

In Jesus' Name, Amen!

CONFESSION:

I claim the promise of God in Mark 16:18–that if there is any deadly substance in my food, water, or medications, it will not hurt me.

PERSONAL THOUGHTS:

_____

_____

_____

_____

_____

_____

_____

_____

_____

_____

_____

_____

_____

_____

_____

_____

_____

_____

_____

DAY 26

Maximizing the Seed of the Word of God

Scriptures:

Mark 4:14-20 New King James Version (NKJV)

¹⁴ The sower sows the word. ¹⁵ And these are the ones by the wayside where the word is sown. When they hear, Satan comes immediately and takes away the word that was sown in their hearts. ¹⁶ These likewise are the ones sown on stony ground who, when they hear the word, immediately receive it with gladness; ¹⁷ and they have no root in themselves, and so endure only for a time. Afterward, when tribulation or persecution arises for the word's sake, immediately they stumble. ¹⁸ Now these are the ones sown among thorns; they are the ones who hear the word, ¹⁹ and the cares of this world, the deceitfulness of riches, and the desires for

*other things entering in choke the word, and
it becomes unfruitful. [20] But these are the ones
sown on good ground, those who hear the word,
accept it, and bear fruit: some thirtyfold, some
sixty, and some a hundred.*

When you hear God's Word concerning health and wholeness, what do you do with it? The answer to this question is
especially important in determining how God's Word will
impact your life. In Mark 4:14-20, Jesus explains a parable
illustrating the Word of God as a seed that a farmer sow. Here,
Jesus describes four types of ground where the seed is sown –
wayside, stony, thorny, and good ground. These grounds represent what people who hear the Word do with the Word. Let's
look at the four types of ground where God's Word concerning
health and wholeness is sown.

For the **wayside ground**, a person hears the Word of God
concerning health and wholeness, but readily dismisses the
Word when Satan suggests, "Surely, you don't think that will
really work to make you healthy and whole? It is just too good
to be true. You can't believe that the stripes that Jesus took on
His body have any effect on your body. That doesn't make
sense." When the person dismisses the Word of God, Satan's
job is done. He now has free reign to operate in that person's
life by stealing, killing, and destroying.

If Satan's suggestion can't influence the person to dismiss
the Word of God, then He will see if this is a **stony ground**
believer. The **stony ground** believer has received the Word

with gladness and is excited about the Word. So, Satan will see if sending affliction and persecution will force the believer give up on the Word. To make the person dismiss the Word concerning health and wholeness, Satan may attack his/her body with symptoms of sickness. **Stony ground** believers hold onto the Word concerning health and wholeness for a little while. If healing does not manifest immediately, they will give up on the Word, saying, "Maybe the Word doesn't really work." Yet again, Satan's job is done.

Now, the **thorny ground** believer received the Word; and, it has taken root in the person's heart. This person may have experienced some victories by standing on the Word for health and wholeness. But, as time goes on, things of the world start to take root in the person's heart and crowds out the Word of God. The Word begins to whither and no longer has an impact on the person's life. When this person's body is attacked by illness, the last thing that he or she will consider is the Word of God. They will try everything the world offers to get well while ignoring God's Word; and this causes the Word to have no effect. While seeking the world's way of doing things, they forget that Jesus is the source for health and wholeness.

Lastly, there are **good ground** believers who receive the Word of God, and by meditating on the Word, the Word forms strong roots in their heart. When their bodies are attacked, they will stand strong on the Word of God concerning health and wholeness. They will refuse to let go of the Word. As a result, God's Word which says, "Jesus took stripes on His body that our bodies may be whole", produces the manifested fruit of health and wholeness in their lives.

PRAYER:

Lord, help me to nourish and cherish the seed of Your Word that it will grow and be deeply rooted in my heart. Help me to be a **good ground** believer so that I will bear the magnificent fruit of Your Word concerning health and wholeness in my life. Thank You, Lord, for Your Word!

I pray this in Jesus' Name. Amen!

CONFESSION:

I am a **good ground** believer of God's Word. I receive, nourish, and cherish the Word so that it will be deeply rooted in my heart. Therefore, whenever I am faced with the storms of affliction and sickness for the Word's sake, I will stand firmly on the Word that by Jesus' stripes, I am healed. I am reaping the harvest of health and wholeness because God's Word is deeply rooted in my heart.

PERSONAL THOUGHTS:

_____

_____

_____

_____

_____

_____

_____

_____

_____

_____

_____

_____

_____

_____

_____

_____

_____

_____

_____

Final Thoughts

DAY 27

Refuse to be Normal

Scriptures:

Psalm 91 (ERV)

You can go to God Most High to hide.
You can go to God All-Powerful for protection.
² I say to the Lord, "You are my place of safety, my fortress.
³ God will save you from hidden dangers
and from deadly diseases.
My God, I trust in you."
⁴ You can go to him for protection.
He will cover you like a bird spreading its wings over its babies.
You can trust him to surround and protect you like a shield.
⁵ You will have nothing to fear at night
and no need to be afraid of enemy arrows during the day.
*⁶ **You will have no fear of diseases** that come in the dark*
or terrible suffering that comes at noon.
⁷ A thousand people may fall dead at your side
or ten thousand right beside you,
but nothing bad will happen to you!

⁸ All you will have to do is watch,
and you will see that the wicked are punished.
⁹ You trust in the Lord for protection.
You have made God Most High your place of safety.
¹⁰ So nothing bad will happen to you.
No diseases will come near your home.
¹¹ He will command his angels to protect you wherever you go.
¹² Their hands will catch you
so that you will not hit your foot on a rock.
¹³ You will have power to trample on lions
and poisonous snakes.
¹⁴ **The Lord says, "If someone trusts me, I will save them.**
I will protect my followers who call to me for help.
¹⁵ When my followers call to me, I will answer them.
I will be with them when they are in trouble.
I will rescue them and honor them.
¹⁶ **I will give my followers a long life**
and show them my power to save."

In our world today, it may look as if it is normal to be burdened with some type of sickness or disease. Faster than medical science can come up with cures, diseases are multiplying. Almost every person you encounter is suffering from some type of illness and is on medication of some kind. What is even more disturbing is that diseases are impacting the lives of people you know personally – people in your family, church, and community. If you allow it, these situations can cause you to fear. You may start thinking, "Why should I believe that I will overcome sickness when most people around me are being victimized by sickness?" According to Psalms 91:7, just because disaster is happening to those around you, it doesn't have to happen to you. If you truly trust in your Father God, disease can impact thousands of people around you, but it will NOT come near you.

I recall, within about a year's time, I lost twelve people who were dear to me. Most of them died from some type of illness. As I was burdened by grief, I began to feel that we were in losing battle against sickness. Thoughts from the enemy began to come to my mind such as, "People around you are being taken out by illnesses; what makes you think you can live a long, healthy life?" I really had to shake myself with the Word of God to keep from feeling overwhelmed and falling into the deception that living a long, healthy life was impossible. I had to continually rehearse the promises of God. In Psalm 91, God made some awesome promises concerning protection from diseases and from anything that would cause us bodily harm. If we truly trust God–that is, believe His Word without doubt–we will receive this protection. Keep in mind, God Almighty made these promises; not a man, but our God, who cannot lie. Read Psalm 91 over and over again and build your **trust** in God. Then, you will see this type of protection manifested in your life. Notice that verses 14 and 16 (ERV) reads: *The Lord says, "If someone **trusts me**, I will save them. I will protect my followers who call to me for help. I will give my followers a long life and show them my power to save."* God wants to give us long, healthy lives to show the world His supernatural power to protect those who truly trust in Him.

Maybe it has become normal for people to be overtaken by sickness and diseases. But you can refuse to be normal. You can stick out like a sore thumb and be different. People may ask, "Why is it that sickness and disease don't overtake you?" The answer is that you trust in the Most-High God for your protection. God has promised in His Word that if thousands of people around you succumb to diseases, no disease can have victory over your life because you put your trust in Him.

PRAYER:

Father God, thank You so much for setting the standard for our lives in Your Word. Your standard is for me to live a long, healthy life. Therefore, I don't have to succumb to what is happening around me. I can live beyond the norm. Lord, help me to develop my spirit to live out Your Word and to help others to do the same. I pray this in the precious Name of Jesus. Amen!

CONFESSION:

Even though it may be normal for people around me to succumb to sicknesses and diseases, I will NOT fear! I trust God's Word which comforts me and helps me to know that if thousands of people around me succumb to sickness, it will NOT overtake me! God has promised me a long, satisfying life; and, I am walking into everything that God has promised me in His Word. I refuse to be normal. I am living a life beyond the norm!

PERSONAL THOUGHTS:

_____

_____

_____

_____

_____

_____

_____

_____

_____

_____

_____

_____

_____

_____

_____

_____

_____

_____

_____

_____

DAY 28

Superhuman

Scriptures:

Ephesians 6:10 (NKJV) – *Finally, my brethren, be strong in the Lord and in the power of His might.*

1 John 4:4 (NKJV) – *You are of God, little children, and have overcome them, because He who is in you is greater than he who is in the world.*

Romans 8:11 (KJV) – *But if the Spirit of him that raised up Jesus from the dead dwell in you, he that raised up Christ from the dead shall also quicken your mortal bodies by his Spirit that dwelleth in you.*

Have you ever watched a superhero movie? The heroes have powers that far exceed the powers of normal human beings. Have you ever thought, "Wouldn't it be awesome to have extraordinary physical and mental powers to help me to succeed in everyday life?" Well, as a born-again believer, YOU DO!

Romans 8:11 declares that we have the same power in us that raised Jesus' body from the dead and that power quickens (makes alive) our mortal human bodies. Just think, we have the SAME POWER–not an alternative power, not a lesser power, but the SAME POWER–that raised Jesus from the dead residing in us! This power adds super to our natural human bodies, making us superhuman.

We can eat healthy, exercise, and do all the things others might do to contribute to a healthy lifestyle. But we have much more that contributes to a healthy life than normal people do. We have the same power that raised Jesus' body from the dead impacting the functioning of our physical mortal bodies. We actually have the Spirit of God, our creator, living in us – the One who is greater than anything or anyone in this world. According to I John 4:4, greater is He who is in us than he who is in the world. We have strength beyond our natural human strength. Ephesian 6:10 admonishes us to be strong in the Lord and in the power of His might. Just think, when our own human strength is not enough, we can tap into HIS MIGHT, that is, the supernatural strength of our Almighty God. How awesome is that!

When we are born-again, we are born into the superhuman family of our Father God. We gain powers and strengths that are far beyond what was provided to us in our natural human birth. Just like we inherit attributes of our human parents, when we are born-again, we inherit attributes of our Father God.

We know that we were born again spiritually. But we must realize that this spiritual birth impacts our whole being – spirit, soul, and body.

Why do born-again people of God live as mere humans, when we have the supernatural power of God in us? I believe the reason is some of us don't know any better. Some are just not aware. According to Hosea 4:6, God's people are destroyed because of the lack of knowledge. But there are those who know what the Word of God says about God's supernatural power in us, yet, they truly don't believe it.

I am convinced that people in the family of God should be the smartest and healthiest people in the world. We have access to the wisdom and might of God. Through the wisdom of God by the leadership of Holy Spirit, we can receive divine directions on things to do in the natural that would make our bodies strong. After we have obeyed the leading of the Holy Spirit on what we need to do naturally to have healthy bodies, we have the supernatural might of God quickening our mortal bodies, making us superhuman. In the Book of Daniel, Daniel and the three Hebrew boys were healthier and smarter than their peers. They were led by the wisdom of God as to what to eat to be naturally healthy, in addition, by the supernatural power of God, the three Hebrew boys' bodies became superhuman to the point that their bodies were able to withstand the fiery furnace. Their bodies became supernaturally fire-resistant. They demonstrated that once we do natural healthy things, there is a power that is beyond the natural that will give our bodies superhuman might.

So, stop living as a mere human. Renew your mind to the truth that we have strength beyond our natural strength. We have the might of God in our mortal bodies. We are strong in the Lord and in the power of His might; and, the same power that raised Jesus' body from the dead resides in our bodies. As born-again believers, we are superhumans!

I am an advocate of eating right, exercising, and doing those natural things for a healthy life. But don't stop there. According to Deuteronomy 8:3, Matthew 4:4 and Luke 4:4, "Man should not live by bread alone but by every Word of God." Yes, we do natural things to be healthy; but, we should also live by God's Word which brings supernatural health and strength to our bodies. Go farther than the natural and tap into the supernatural power that is in you to quicken your mortal body and take your body to another level of health that is beyond the norm.

What if we go to heaven and realize the type of life we could have lived? Jesus may say, "I gave you my power and authority over all the works of the devil so that nothing would be able to hurt you. I put my spirit in you which was the same power that raised my body from the dead to quicken your mortal body with youth-renewing power. Why did you fear? Why did you succumb to sickness, disease, and weakness? I gave you My might so that you would not be weak. Why did you live like a mere human when I made you superhuman?"

We are surrounded by people who live as mere humans. Many Christians think they are mere humans. According to Proverbs 23:7, as a person thinks in his heart, so is he. A person's perception becomes his/her reality. It is like the story of an eagle surrounded by chickens. The eagle becomes like the chickens because it thinks it is a chicken; so, it never uses the power that is within it to soar.

Romans 12:2 Modern English Version (MEV) states:

"Do not be conformed to this world, but be trans-formed by the renewing of your mind, that you may prove what is the good and acceptable and perfect will of God."

The eagle conformed to its surroundings. Many Christians are conforming to the world's way of thinking; so, like the eagle, they will never soar into walking out the perfect will of God for their lives. They are becoming just like the people who are around them: mere humans. It takes effort to be trans-formed. It takes effort to renew your mind on what God's Word says about you. It takes no effort to conform and think the way others around you are thinking. When we conform to the world's way of thinking, we come so short of God's glory. God wants to manifest Himself in us and through us. When we con-form to thinking like everyone else, God can't show His glory through us and demonstrate to the world that there is a super-natural way to live. Habakkuk 2:4, Romans 1:17, Galatians 3:11 and Hebrews 10:38 all state, "The just shall live by faith." We must renew our minds to be able to live by faith. We can't think like the world and maintain our faith. We can only live this supernatural life by faith. Faith is simply believing God's Word beyond the words of any other. To not be deceived, we must put our faith in God's Word. According to Revelations 12:9, "... that old serpent, called the Devil, and Satan, which deceiveth the whole world..." The world is deceived, and if we conform to the world's way of thinking, we also will be deceived.

Jesus is our greatest example of a superhuman. He dominated sickness, diseases, and evil spirits. He took authority over destructive storms and defied natural laws by walking on water and feeding 5,000 people with a few fish and loaves of bread. You might say, "Sure, Jesus was superhuman because he was the son of God." While Jesus was on the earth, He identified Himself as the Son of man. Jesus wanted us to be fully aware that while in His earthly body, He operated as human. He was not just a mere human, though; he was a human whose body was indwelled by the Holy Spirit. It was the Holy Spirit within Jesus who caused Him to live a superhuman life. As born-again believers, our bodies are the temple of the Holy Spirit. The Holy Spirit indwells our bodies just as He indwelled Jesus' earthly body. So, we, too, can live superhuman lives. We can live beyond the norm.

CONFESSION:

When I was born-again, I was born into a superhuman family with Almighty God as my Father. I have the very nature of my Father God in me. Therefore, I am not just a mere human. I am superhuman.

- I have wisdom that others don't have. I have the mind of Christ.
- I have strength and might that others don't have. I am strong in the LORD and the power of His might.
- I walk in supernatural health and wholeness. My body is the temple of the Holy Spirit; and, the same Spirit that raised Jesus' body from the dead is in me, quickening my mortal body and making my mortal body operate in a superhuman mode.

I AM SUPERHUMAN!

PRAYER:

Lord, help me to walk as the new creature that You created me to be at my new birth. Help me to walk in Your supernatural power that is now a part of my very being. I know that the idea of being superhuman is far fetch to most. But help this to be my reality. Help this to be the reality for Your children, so that we will not succumb to living as mere humans when You have made us superhuman. I pray this in Jesus' Name. AMEN!

PERSONAL THOUGHTS:

_____

_____

_____

_____

_____

_____

_____

_____

_____

_____

_____

_____

_____

_____

_____

_____

_____

_____

_____

_____

CONCLUSION

I hope that by reading this book, your thinking has changed, and you realize that God desires for you to walk in health and wholeness that is beyond what most people experience.

In this book, God gave us great revelations on living in health and wholeness that is beyond the norm. I truly believe there is much more yet to be revealed. Therefore, I am continuing my pursuit of wisdom from God on this subject. I suggest that you do the same. God does not want us to be in darkness about anything concerning His will for our lives. He has promised to reveal things to us by the Holy Spirit which lives on the inside of every born-again believer. I pray for great success in your personal pursuit of wisdom from God concerning living a life beyond the norm.

We acknowledged that there are natural practical things to do to promote a healthy lifestyle. But more than just the natural, this book focuses on adding "the God factor" to our lifestyle. To walk out God's plan for a healthy and whole life, we must develop our personal relationship with our Father God through Christ Jesus, proclaim the Word of God, seek the wisdom of God, and be led by the Holy Spirit. "The God factor" is what makes this book different from many other books on health and wholeness. God does make a difference! Inviting Him into any area of our lives makes all the difference in the world. Human wisdom and natural willpower will take us only so far. But adding "the God factor" can take us far beyond the norm into the divine health and wholeness that God desires for us.

It is not only God's desire for us to be healthy and whole, but God also needs us to be healthy and whole. God has work for us to do. He has Kingdom business for us to take care of. He has people He wants us to be a blessing to. He wants us to be well so we can help others to be well. You see, God wants our lives, as born-again believers, to manifest the redemptive work of Jesus, so that we can be examples of the type of life that Jesus suffered and died for us to have. Somebody needs to walk out the life of supernatural health and wholeness that Jesus purchased for us. Why not let it be you? Somebody needs to demonstrate that God has equipped us to live lives that are beyond the norm. Why not let it be you?

Prayer for the Reader

It is my prayer that by reading this book, your life will be forever changed by:

- Opening the eyes of your understanding to the truth of God's Word concerning health and wholeness.
- Encouraging you to seek God's wisdom through the leadership of the Holy Spirit for practical things to do to promote health and wholeness.
- Being aware of and using the God-given tools for living a life of divine health and wholeness.
- Inspiring you to be determined to pursue a lifestyle of divine health and wholeness and never settle for anything less.
- Building within you, unshakeable faith in the reality that God wants you to well and that Jesus came so you can have an abundant life.

I pray that this book will inspire you to continue your personal pursuit of greater wisdom from God, and that you will be instrumental in motiving others to live lives of divine health and wholeness. As a result, the true believers in Jesus will be signs and wonders to the world, demonstrating God's will and ability to heal, make whole and equip people to live in health and wholeness that is beyond the norm.

Be blessed in your spirit, soul, and body!

I pray this in Jesus' Name. Amen!

Confession for the Reader

By the leadership of the Holy Spirit who lives in me, I am applying the principles in the Word of God concerning health and wholeness to my life. In doing so, I am living a life of health and wholeness that is beyond what most people experience. I am living the abundant life that Jesus provided for me. I maintain a healthy lifestyle by making adjustments to my health habits through the leadership of the Holy Spirit; eliminating stress by keeping my mind on the Word of God which gives me a peace that is beyond human understanding; and, maintaining a joyful heart by praising my Father God at all times.

If I am attacked with symptoms of sickness, my heart is fixed, trusting in God's Word. From God's Word, I know that by Jesus' stripes I am healed; no weapon formed against me can prosper; the same power that raised Jesus' body from the dead is impacting my mortal body; the Blood of Jesus has redeemed me from the curse of sickness; and, physical evidence must line up with the unchanging truth of God's Word.

In the NAME OF JESUS and by the power of the HOLY SPIRIT, I am walking in supernatural health and wholeness and living a long satisfying life that is far beyond the norm.

Prayer for Salvation and Baptism in the Holy Spirit

To seek wisdom, you must be connected to the source of wisdom – the Almighty God. The first step to walking in divine health and wholeness is to establish a relationship with God, your creator, by accepting Jesus as your savior. If you have not already established this relationship, I suggest that you take this opportunity to start a fresh, new relationship with the Almighty God. If you can sincerely say the following with no reservations, you will start a new relationship with God as your loving Father.

> **Dear God, thank You for loving me so much that You allowed Your Son Jesus to die on the cross to pay the penalty for my sin, enabling me to be connected to You. I accept Jesus as my Lord and Savior. I praise You that I am born again into Your family with You as my Father. As your child, according to Luke 11:13, You will give me Your Holy Spirit, if I ask. Therefore, I now ask that You fill me with Your Holy Spirit. I receive the infilling of Your Holy Spirit. Since I am filled with the Holy Spirit, I expect to speak with other tongues as the Holy Spirit gives me the utterance as described in Act 2:4. I expect the Holy Spirit to lead me, guide me, and give me wisdom to fulfill Your divine will for my life. I pray this in Jesus' Name. Amen.**

By believing in your heart what you just confessed in this prayer, you have been born again. As a human, you are a three-part being – spirit, soul, and body. You are a spirit, you have a soul (mind, will, and emotions), and you live in a body. By being born again, your spirit has been made complete, and you are born into the family of God where God is now your Father. Your spirit is now brand new, causing you to have a divine connection with your Father God. You now have traits of your Father. You have His nature in your born-again spirit.

You are now filled with the Holy Spirit. The Holy Spirit has given you a language to use during your prayer time that enables you to pray beyond your natural understanding. As you pray, you are now able to tap into the perfect wisdom of God concerning any situation.

When we speak of divine health and wholeness, we are speaking of health and wholeness to your whole person – spirit, soul, and body. Now that your spirit has been made whole through your new birth and you are filled with the Holy Spirit, the Word of God and the Holy Spirit will assist you in bringing wholeness to your soul and body. When your spirit, soul and body are in harmony, you will walk in the divine health and wholeness that God intends for you.

Summary of Scriptures for Divine Health and Wholeness

Isaiah 53:4-5 Common English Bible (CEB)–It was certainly our sickness that he carried, and our sufferings that he bore, but we thought him afflicted, struck down by God and tormented.

⁵He was pierced because of our rebellions and crushed because of our crimes. **He bore the punishment that made us whole; by his wounds we are healed.**

1 Peter 2:24 Good News Translation (GNT)–Christ himself carried our sins in his body to the cross, so that we might die to sin and live for righteousness. **It is by his wounds that you have been healed.**

1 Corinthians 6:19, Romans 8:11, New Living Translation (NLT)–Don't you realize that your body is the temple of the Holy Spirit, who lives in you and was given to you by God? You do not belong to yourself. The Spirit of God, who raised Jesus from the dead, lives in you. **And just as God raised Christ Jesus from the dead, he will give life to your mortal bodies** by this same Spirit living within you.

1 John 4:4 (NKJV) – You are of God, … He who is in you is greater than he who is in the world.

John 10:10–Amplified Bible (AMP) … I came that they may have *and* enjoy life, and have it in abundance [to the full, till it overflows].

Romans 12:1 (KJV)–I beseech you therefore, brethren by the mercies of God, that you present your bodies a living sacrifice, holy, acceptable unto God, which is your reasonable service.

Proverbs 3:5-8 The Passion Translation (TPT)–Trust in the Lord completely, and do not rely on your own opinions. With all your heart rely on him to guide you, and he will lead you in every decision you make. [6] **Become intimate with him in whatever you do**, and he will lead you wherever you go. [7] Don't think for a moment that you know it all, **for wisdom comes when you adore him with undivided devotion** and avoid everything that's wrong.[8] **Then you will find the healing refreshment your body and spirit long for.**

Psalm 16:11 (KJV) -Thou wilt shew me the path of life: **in thy presence is fulness of joy**; at thy right hand there are pleasures for evermore.

Proverbs 18:21 Good News Translation (GNT)–What you say can preserve life or destroy it; so you must accept the consequences of your words.

John 14:26 Amplified Bible (AMP)—But the Helper (Comforter, Advocate, Intercessor—Counselor, Strengthener, Standby), the Holy Spirit, whom the Father will send in My name [in My place, to represent Me and act on My behalf], He will teach you all things. And He will help you remember everything that I have told you.

Romans 8:13 (KJV) – For if ye live after the flesh, ye shall die: but if ye through the Spirit do mortify the deeds of the body, ye shall live.

1 Timothy 4:8 Good News Translation (GNT)—Physical exercise has some value ...

Deuteronomy 25:15 – But thou shalt have a perfect and just weight, a perfect and just measure shall thou have: that thy days may be lengthened in the land which the Lord thy God giveth thee.

Proverbs 3:24 (VOICE)—Your mind will be clear, free from fear; when you lie down to rest, you will be refreshed by sweet sleep.

Hebrews 4:9-11 The Passion Translation (TPT)—So we conclude that there is still a full and complete "rest" waiting for believers to experience. [10] As we enter into God's faith-rest life we cease from our own works, just as God celebrates his finished works and rests in them. [11] So then we must give our all and be eager to experience this faith-rest life, so that no one falls short by following the same pattern of doubt and unbelief.

John 5:19 Contemporary English Version (CEV)–Jesus told the people: I tell you for certain that the Son cannot do anything on his own. He can do only what he sees the Father doing, and he does exactly what he sees the Father do.

Psalm 91:14-16 Amplified Bible (AMP)–[14]Because he set his love on Me, therefore I will save him; I will set him [securely] on high, because he knows My name [he confidently trusts and relies on Me, knowing I will never abandon him, no, never]. [15] He will call upon Me, and I will answer him; I will be with him in trouble; I will rescue him and honor him. [16] "With **a long life I will satisfy him;** And I will let him see My salvation.

Proverbs 3:1-2 New Living Translation (NLT)–My child, never forget the things I have taught you. Store my commands in your heart. [2] If you do this, **you will live many years, and your life will be satisfying.**

Romans 8:37 The Passion Translation (TPT)–Yet even in the midst of all these things, we triumph over them all, for **God has made us to be more than conquerors,** and his demonstrated love is our glorious victory over everything!

Luke 18:1, 8 (AMP)–Also [Jesus] told them a parable to the effect that they ought always to pray and not to turn coward (faint, lose heart, and give up). I tell you, He will defend and protect and avenge them speedily. However, will He find [persistence in] faith in the earth?

Psalm 34:1 (KJV)–I will bless the Lord at all times: his praise shall continually be in my mouth.

Psalm 69:30 Good News Translation (GNT)–I will praise God with a song; I will proclaim his greatness by giving him thanks.

Psalm 106:1 (KJV)–Praise ye the Lord. O give thanks unto the Lord; for he is good: for his mercy endureth for ever.

Isaiah 25:1 Good News Translation (GNT)–Lord, you are my God; I will honor you and praise your name. You have done amazing things; you have faithfully carried out the plans you made long ago.

Deuteronomy 10:21 Good News Translation (GNT)–Praise him—he is your God, and you have seen with your own eyes the great and astounding things that he has done for you.

Psalm 103:1-5 New Living Translation (NLT)–Let all that I am praise the Lord; with my whole heart, I will praise his holy name. ² Let all that I am praise the Lord; may I never forget the good things he does for me. ³ He forgives all my sins and heals all my diseases. ⁴ He redeems me from death and crowns me with love and tender mercies. [5] He fills my life with good things. My youth is renewed like the eagle's!

Proverbs 17:22 Good News Translation (GNT)–Being cheerful keeps you healthy. It is slow death to be gloomy all the time.

Nehemiah 8:10 (KJV)–… the joy of the Lord is your strength.

Matthew 7:24 The Passion Translation (TPT)–Everyone who hears my teaching and applies it to his life can be compared to a wise man who built his house on an unshakable foundation.

2 Corinthians 4:18 (KJV)–While we look not at the things which are seen, but at the things which are not seen: for the things which are seen are temporal; but the things which are not seen are eternal.

2 Corinthians 5:7 (KJV)–(For we walk by faith, not by sight:)

Numbers 23:19 New Life Version (NLV)–God is not a man, that He should lie. He is not a son of man, that He should be sorry for what He has said. Has He said, and will He not do it? Has He spoken, and will He not keep His Word?

John 8:32 Modern English Version (MEV)–You shall know the truth, and the truth shall set you free.

Hebrews 11:6 (KJV)–But without faith it is impossible to please him: for he that cometh to God must believe that he is, and that he is a rewarder of them that diligently seek him.

James 1:6-7 New Living Translation (NLT)–But when you ask him, be sure that your faith is in God alone. Do not waver, for a person with divided loyalty is as unsettled as a wave of the sea that is blown and tossed by the wind. ⁷ Such people should not expect to receive anything from the Lord.

Psalm 91:7 (NKJV)–A thousand may fall at your side, and ten thousand at your right hand; But it shall not come near you.

Mark 16:17-18–And these signs shall follow them that believe … if they drink any deadly thing, it shall not hurt them.

Psalms 103:2 and 5 (KJV)–Bless the LORD, O my soul, and forget not all his benefits: Who satisfieth thy mouth with good things; so that thy youth is renewed like the eagle's.

2 Timothy 1:7 (KJV)–For God hath not given us the spirit of fear; but of power, and of love, and of a sound mind.

Philippians 4:6,7 Living Bible (TLB)–⁶ Don't worry about anything; instead, pray about everything; tell God your needs, and don't forget to thank him for his answers. ⁷ If you do this, you will experience God's peace, which is far more wonderful than the human mind can understand. His peace will keep your thoughts and your hearts quiet and at rest as you trust in Christ Jesus.

John 14:27 (KJV)–[27] Peace I leave with you, my peace I give unto you: not as the world giveth, give I unto you. Let not your heart be troubled, neither let it be afraid.

Isaiah 26:3 (KJV)–Thou wilt keep him in perfect peace, whose mind is stayed on thee: because he trusteth in thee.

1 Peter 5:7 (KJV)–[7] Casting all your care upon him; for he careth for you.

Ephesians 4:32 The Message (MSG) … Be gentle with one another, sensitive. Forgive one another as quickly and thoroughly as God in Christ forgave you.

Matthew 5:44 (KJV)–I say unto you, Love your enemies, bless them that curse you, do good to them that hate you, and pray for them which despitefully use you, and persecute you;

Romans 12:20 (KJV)–Therefore if thine enemy hunger, feed him; if he thirst, give him drink: for in so doing thou shalt heap coals of fire on his head.

Ephesians 6:10 (NKJV) – Finally, my brethren, be strong in the Lord and in the power of His might.

Proverbs 4:20-22 (TPT)–Listen carefully, my dear child, to everything that I teach you, and pay attention to all that I have to say. [21] Fill your thoughts with my words until they penetrate deep into your spirit. [22] Then, as you unwrap my words, they will impart true life and radiant health into the very core of your being.

Matthew 9:29 (KJV)–… According to your faith be it unto you.

Bible References